Civil Aviation

IN NORTHERN IRELAND

An Illustrated History – 1909 to the Present Day

GUY WARNER & ERNIE CROMIE

COLOURPOINT BOOKS

Published 2013 by Colourpoint Books
An imprint of Colourpoint Creative Ltd
Colourpoint House, Jubilee Business Park
Jubilee Road, Newtownards, BT23 4YH
Tel: 028 9182 6339
Fax: 028 9182 1900
E-mail: info@colourpoint.co.uk
Web: www.colourpoint.co.uk

First Edition
First Impression

A catalogue record for this book is available from the British Library.

Designed by April Sky Design, Newtownards
Tel: 028 9182 7195 • Web: www.aprilsky.co.uk

Printed by GPS Colour Graphics Ltd, Belfast

ISBN 978-1-78073-048-6

Front cover: G-APEF, the first BEA Vanguard to land at Aldergrove on 25 September 1963 – a diversion from Nutts Corner because of bad weather. *(Joe Brown)*
Small images (l-r): The muddy conditions at the pioneering airfield established at Malone in Belfast. *(Cobham plc)*
Spartan II Cruiser, G-ACZM, at Ards Airport in the 1930s. *(Ernie Cromie Collection)*
A postcard bought at Nutts Corner in 1962 depicting a Viscount 736 from the mid-1950s. *(Ernie Cromie Collection)*

Rear cover: Airbus A319, G-EUPC, of British Airways arrives with the Olympic flame at GBBCA on 2 June 2012. *(GBBCA)*
Emerald Airways DH Heron, G-ALZL, at Eglinton. *(Hugh McGratton)*
BA (Brymon) Dash-8, G-BRYS, at Enniskillen. *(Gerry Gallagher)*

CONTENTS

ABOUT THE AUTHORS

Guy Warner is a retired schoolteacher and former civil servant, who grew up in Newtownabbey, attending Abbots Cross Primary School and Belfast High School before going to Leicester University and later Stranmillis College. He now lives in Greenisland, Co Antrim with his wife Lynda. He is the author of more than 20 books and booklets on aviation and has written a large number of articles for magazines in the UK, Ireland and the USA. He also reviews books for several publications, gives talks to local history societies, etc and has appeared on TV and radio programmes, discussing aspects of aviation history. He is the Vice-Chairman of the Ulster Aviation Society – for more information about the Society please see: www.ulsteraviationsociety.org

Ernie Cromie's almost lifelong interest in all things aeronautical was initially inspired by the sight and sound of a Royal Air Force Halifax bomber from the Meteorological Squadron at Aldergrove circling over farm livestock trapped by deep snow drifts around his home, in the foothills of Slieve Croob in Co Down, during the unforgettably bad winter of 1947. Twelve years later, when he was a member of the Army Cadet Force, his first-ever flight was in a RAF Anson aircraft at Jurby, Isle of Man. Unable to realise his boyhood ambition to become a pilot in the RAF because of defective eyesight, he had a fulfilling career as a town planner in the Northern Ireland Civil Service but never lost his enthusiasm for all things aviation. He has been a member of the Ulster Aviation Society since 1979, serving as its Chairman for 30 years until 2012 when he relinquished all executive responsibility in order to devote more time to researching the history of aviation in Northern Ireland, with particular reference to the United States Army Air Force and Naval Air Service presence there during the Second World War. He has written numerous articles for a wide range of aviation journals and other publications, and this is his second book.

If this book encourages you to take a deeper interest in aviation in Northern Ireland, past and present, you may wish to join the **Ulster Aviation Society**. You can explore the information, history, events and aircraft owned by the society at:

www.ulsteraviationsociety.org

FOREWORD

ALONG WITH THE mobile phone and the laptop, the convenience of air travel is one of the innovations that have marked the consumer revolution of the jet age.

We take it more or less for granted that we can have breakfast at home and lunch or dinner in another country in less than 24 hours. Flying has become as second nature as getting on a bus or train and the advent of package holidays and budget airlines has combined to bring prices well within the reach of most pockets.

Access from your own front door is now even easier with the three service hubs at Belfast International, George Best City Airport and City of Derry combining to offer wider customer choice.

The importance of low cost air travel is a key priority for the Stormont administration. That is why, on 6 November 2012, the Northern Ireland Executive fulfilled its Programme for Government pledge to axe Air Passenger Duty on all outward bound long haul flights. In doing this we have helped the local economy by boosting our competitiveness and reducing cost to both the inward investor and the tourist.

As a fast means of getting from A to B flying has no rivals but, when talking to some of our older citizens, there is a sense that the experience has lost some of its uniqueness.

Many recall the little 'garden' area in front of the cosy departure lounge at Nutts Corner with only a low privet hedge separating spectators from the parked 'Pionairs' a few metres away. Others remember the novelty of a family day out to 'Aldergrove' in the mid-1960s where a pleasant afternoon could be spent people watching and plane spotting.

For those who flew, the recollection of stewardesses and their silver trays of barley sugar to help stop your ears popping is what remains most vivid.

Time flies, just like the rest of us.

RT HON PETER D ROBINSON MLA
First Minister

MARTIN McGUINNESS MLA
deputy First Minister

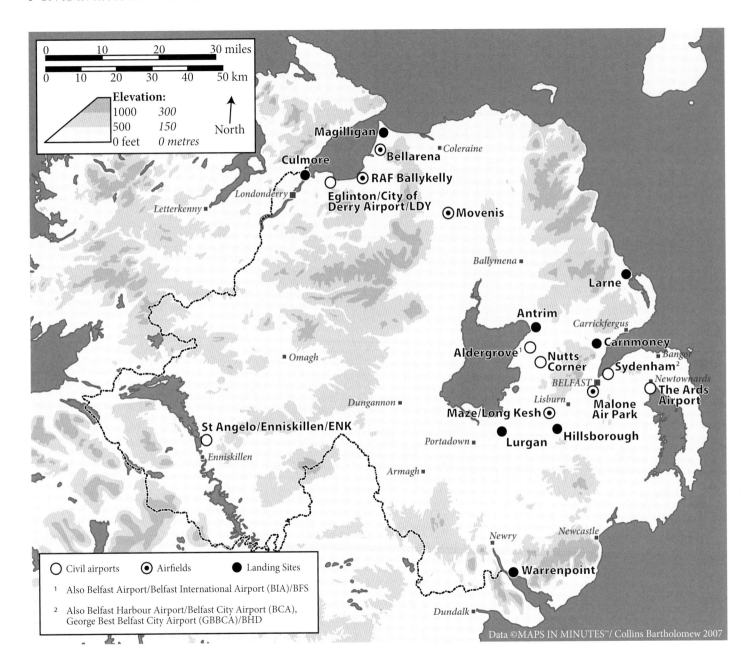

0   10   20   30 miles

0   10   20   30   40   50 km

Elevation:

1000	*300*
500	*150*
0 feet	*0 metres*

North

Magilligan

Bellarena

Culmore

■ *Coleraine*

RAF Ballykelly

Londonderry ■

**Eglinton/City of
Derry Airport/LDY**

Letterkenny ■

Movenis

Ballymena ■

Larne

Antrim

Carrickfergus ■

Aldergrove[1]

Carnmoney

■ Omagh

Nutts
Corner

Sydenham[2]

■ *Bangor*

BELFAST ■

Newtownards ■

**The Ards
Airport**

Dungannon ■

Lisburn ■

Malone
Air Park

Maze/Long Kesh

St Angelo/Enniskillen/ENK

Portadown ■

Lurgan

Hillsborough

Enniskillen ■

Armagh ■

Newry ■

Newcastle ■

Warrenpoint

Dundalk ■

○ Civil airports   ◉ Airfields   ● Landing Sites

[1] Also Belfast Airport/Belfast International Airport (BIA)/BFS

[2] Also Belfast Harbour Airport/Belfast City Airport (BCA),
George Best Belfast City Airport (GBBCA)/BHD

INTRODUCTION

THE SECOND PART of this trilogy concerns the story of civil aviation in Northern Ireland and for the most part deals with powered heavier-than-air flight in the 20th and 21st centuries. However, in the 19th century aviation began in Ulster in the shape of lighter-than-air craft, with the first recorded balloon ascent apparently taking place in 1848, 'when a man called Greer took off from Botanic Gardens and descended somewhere near Craigavad.' One very notable flight took place some 17 years later and received extensive coverage in the press. The Belfast newspaper, the *Northern Whig*, reported in July 1865:

Frightful Balloon Disaster

On Monday July 3rd the balloon ascent of Mr Henry Coxwell, the aeronaut, took place from the Royal Botanic Gardens, Belfast. The 'Research', the name given to the balloon, is the largest aerial machine ever constructed and when inflated presents a very handsome as well as gigantic appearance. It is painted a light brown colour, relieved round the centre with devices in yellow and the words 'Coxwell's Research'. It was purchased by public subscription and presented to Mr Coxwell by a committee of scientific gentlemen. Probably some 10,000 to 12,000 people were in the gardens and the open and beautiful sward in front of the conservatory presented a most animated appearance with the moving throng of well-dressed ladies and gentlemen. At a quarter to six the monster rose in the air.

One of the passengers, of whom some accounts say there were as many as 10, later recalled:

The wind, which was very light carried us over the town

in a northerly direction and the Linenhall, barracks, courthouse, gaol etc were clearly seen but at the height we had attained appeared of the smallest dimensions. Passing over the Cave Hill the view was really magnificent; Belfast, Larne and Strangford Loughs were clearly seen and Lough Neagh, though rather dim from a haze over it. The wind, ever capricious, drove us for a short time inland and it was thought our resting place would be Ballymena but another change took us for Glenarm Bay.

Coxwell intended to make the descent there but a valve at the top of the balloon malfunctioned, with the result that the balloon went out of any form of control and began "bumping with considerable force against the side of the hills above Carnlough for nearly a mile." One of the passengers suffered broken ribs and others were bruised and buffeted. As the shaking grew worse, the occupants realised their peril and began to jump out, but two did not and were carried upwards by the runaway balloon. The others ran after it but could not catch it as it carried "Mr Runge, a German and Mr Halferty of Londonderry" away. Luckily they survived, after a nightmare ride of some 20 miles. Runge later told his story of the events of that memorable but terrifying day:

He entirely exonerated Coxwell from any blame, attributing his mischances solely to the 'reprehensible conduct' of his companions. On approaching the ground, Coxwell gave clear instructions for the passengers to sit down in an unconstrained position facing each other and to be prepared for some heavy shocks. Above all things they were to be careful to get out one by one, and on no account leave hold of the car. Many of the passengers refused to sit down, and, according to Runge, 'behaved in the wildest manner, losing completely their self-control. Seizing the valve rope themselves, they tore it away from its attachment, the stronger pushing back the weaker, and refusing to lend help when they had got out'. Accordingly the car, relieved of their weight, tore away from the grasp of Coxwell and those who still clung to it, rising above the trees, with Runge and Halferty within. As the balloon descended again, they shouted to the countrymen below for succour, but to no avail, and presently, the anchor catching, the car struck the earth with a shock which threw Halferty out on the ground, leaving Runge to rise again into the air, this time alone. He later recalled, 'The balloon moved on in a horizontal direction straight towards the sea. Coming to a farm, I shouted out to the people standing there. Some women, with their quick humane instincts, perceived my danger and exhorted the men to hurry to my assistance, they themselves running as fast as they could to tender what little help they might be able to give me. The anchor stuck in a willow tree. I shouted out to the people below to secure the cable and anchor which they did. The evening was now beautifully still, the breeze had died away, and the balloon was swinging calmly at her moorings above the farmhouse. One of the men asked me whether I had a rope with me, and how I intended to get out. I told them only to take care of the cable, because the balloon would settle down by herself before long. I was congratulating myself on a speedy escape from my dangerous position. I had not counted on the wind. A breeze sprang up, tossed the balloon about like a large sail and the anchor was loose again. It tore through the trees, flinging limbs and branches about like matches. It struck the roof of the farmhouse, splintering the chimneys and tiles like glass. On I went, I came near another farm, shouted out for help and told the men to secure the anchor

to the foot of a large tree close by. The anchor was soon made fast, but this was only a momentary relief. The breeze again filled the half-empty balloon, there was a severe strain on the cable, then a dull sound and a severe concussion of the basket. The cable had broken and the anchor, my last and only hope, was gone. I was now carried straight towards the sea, which was but a short distance ahead. I gave up all hope, sat down resigned in the car, and prepared for the end. Then I discovered that a side current was drifting me towards the mountain; the car struck the ground, and dashed along at a fearful rate, knocking down stone fences and breaking everything it came in contact with in its wild career. By-and-by the knocks became less frequent. We were passing over cultivated country, and the car was skimming the surface and grazing the top of the hedges. I saw a thick hawthorn hedge at some distance before me, and the balloon rapidly sweeping towards it. That was my only chance. I rushed to the edge of the car and flung myself down upon the hedge'. The balloon was later found wrecked on the Isle of Islay, with four coats, two hats and the July 1 edition of the *Northern Whig* being found amidst the debris.

So it may be said that from its earliest beginnings, civil flying was not for the faint-hearted. Moving forward in time, it is a quite remarkable fact that more than 150 million passengers have arrived at or departed from Northern Ireland's civil airports between the 1920s and the present day, with nearly seven million travelling in the last year alone. This history attempts to chronicle and explain how that was achieved.

Ernie Cromie, Hillsborough
Guy Warner, Carrickfergus

Sitting on a sand hill at Magilligan, Rita Marr is on the far left of the photograph, Harry Ferguson reclines to her left. *(Edward Marr)*

Harry Ferguson and his intrepid passenger, Rita Marr. *(Edward Marr)*

Viewing the Ferguson Monoplane on the Strand at Magilligan in 1910. *(Edward Marr)*

It can be argued that the first step in civil aviation was taken on 22 August 1910, a full decade before the foundation of Northern Ireland. Miss Rita Marr, a brave lady from Liverpool, consented to be taken aloft from Magilligan Strand, Co Londonderry by a young Ulsterman from Growell, Co Down, Harry Ferguson, in the fourth variant of a monoplane which he had designed and built himself. Harry, the first Irishman to do so, had first flown successfully on

31 December 1909, at Hillsborough, near Growell. Rita's father was Edward Marr who photographed the scene at Magilligan. He was the son of Lawrence Marr (L Marr and Son) which is still in operation as a Civil Engineering business in Liverpool. It is not believed that the two other aviation pioneers of this period, Lilian Bland or Joseph Cordner, were ever accompanied by passengers on their pioneering flights.

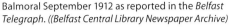

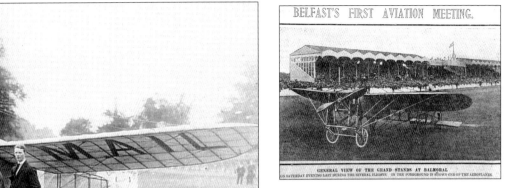

BELFAST'S FIRST AVIATION MEETING.

GENERAL VIEW OF THE GRAND STANDS AT BALMORAL
ON SATURDAY EVENING LAST DURING THE SEVERAL FLIGHTS. IN THE FOREGROUND IS SHOWN ONE OF THE AEROPLANES.

Henri Salmet at Lurgan. *(Ernie Cromie Collection)*

The wreckage of Henry Astley's aeroplane.
(Ulster Aviation Society)

The next four years before the outbreak of the First World War brought a number of daring record breakers and showmen to perform aerial feats which were reported in the local press. They included in 1910: the self-styled 'Captain' Cecil Clayton (no Royal Aero Club Certificate) who exhibited his 30 hp Blériot monoplane at the Ballymoney Show at the end of June and James Radley (RAeC Certificate holder No 12, 14 June 1910) at Bangor in July, with a 25 hp Blériot, who took off in poor weather as the crowd was demanding that he should fly but unfortunately almost immediately crashed into a tree. In June 1910 Clayton's aeroplane had run amok on the ground during an exhibition at Worcester, resulting in the death of a spectator. *Flight* magazine consequently called for greater regulation of airmen performing at public events. Great interest was inspired on 9 September 1912 by the Air Race from Leopardstown to Belfast, organised by the Aero Club of Ireland (founded on 11 November 1909 in Dublin with members including such luminaries as Harry Ferguson, John Boyd Dunlop and John Moore-Brabazon).

The race was ruined by the weather and resulted in most of the 16 original entries deciding not to take part. Of the few who started, only two, HJD Astley (RAeC Certificate No 48, 24 January 1911) in a 70 hp Blériot and James Valentine, (RAeC Certificate No 47, 17 January 1911) flying a 50 hp Deperdussin, got as far as Newry, some 40 miles short of their destination. To compensate, two aviation meetings at Balmoral in Belfast were hastily arranged; to feature Astley, Valentine and the French pilot, Henri Salmet (RAeC Certificate No 99, 27 June 1911), who had already made an appearance in Ulster a few days earlier at the Public Park in Lurgan, under the auspices of the Agricultural and Recreation Association. Tragedy was to follow. On 21 September Henry Astley was killed while flying at Balmoral. He was not wearing a flying helmet, which it was believed might have saved his life. Between 10 and 12 thousand spectators had gathered to witness the flying displays. Astley was 31 years old. He was the 21st British aviator to die in a flying accident and the first fatality in Ireland.

Ronald Whitehouse and his Handley Page at Lurgan in August 1913. *(Belfast Central Library Newspaper Archive)*

Harry Hawker on Larne Lough in 1913. *(Larne Borough Council)*

There were no further performances until August 1913 when Ronald Whitehouse (RAeC Certificate No 407, 21 January 1913) was engaged to fly his Handley Page Type E 50 hp monoplane at the Lurgan Agricultural Show. This was something of an anticlimax as owing to engine trouble the only flight of the day was severely curtailed and the promised joy-rides at two guineas a time never materialised. As was the case with the preceding pilots, he had not flown across from Great Britain but had brought his aeroplane over on the steamer. However, history was made later in the month, when the great airman, Harry Hawker (RAeC Certificate No 297, 17 September 1912) and his mechanic Mr H Kauper, became the first men to fly across the North Channel to Ulster. They were taking part in a round-Britain flight for a prize of £5000 offered by the *Daily Mail*. Hawker's aircraft was a Sopwith HT (Hydro Tractor) Biplane Seaplane. On 27 August he flew from Oban to Larne Harbour, where he refuelled before setting out for Dublin. Further down the coast the aeroplane was observed over Whitehead crossing the mouth of Belfast Lough in the direction of Donaghadee. Spectators witnessed 'the waterplane in full flight' from vantage points in Carrickfergus and Bangor. By 12.15 pm Hawker was passing over Ardglass. Unfortunately mechanical problems induced a forced landing in the sea off the Irish coast at about 2.00 pm, only 13 miles from Dublin, in which the aeroplane was broken up, luckily without life-threatening injury to Hawker or Kauper.

Raynham's Avro 504 at Warrenpoint in 1914.
(Ernie Cromie Collection)

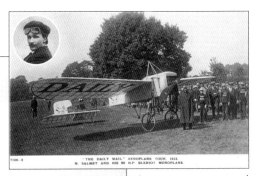

A contemporary postcard featuring Henri Salmet and his 80 hp Blériot.
(via Colin Cruddas)

Henri Salmet and his Blériot on the beach at Ballyholme.
(BELUM.Y.W.05.15.57 © National Museums Northern Ireland Collection Ulster Museum)

On 27 June 1914, Henri Salmet (by then the Chief Instructor at the Blériot Flying School at Hendon) returned to Ulster with Mr FP Raynham (the AV Roe test pilot, RAeC Certificate No 85, 9 May 1911), flying two aircraft, a Blériot and an Avro 504 floatplane – the prototype of this famous aircraft which had been purchased by the *Daily Mail* and fitted with interchangeable floats for a nationwide tour. They displayed them at several locations, including Lurgan and Warrenpoint. *Flight* magazine reported that in Lurgan Raynham started from a small pond while Salmet flew from an adjoining field and added, "In spite of the fact that the whole place was surrounded by trees, making it difficult to get out, both pilots carried a good many passengers during the day." They then flew 25 miles to Warrenpoint, "Raynham followed the

canal from Portadown and took exactly an hour, but during half the journey his motor was only firing on five cylinders and he flew low down between the hills; there was also a strong wind blowing." At Warrenpoint Salmet flew from the Golf Links and Raynham from the Bay. One of Raynham's passengers was Lex Fisher, aged 6½, who thoroughly enjoyed his flight and wanted to go up again. Salmet also appeared at Bangor on 18–19 June, in front of a huge crowd. Special trains had been laid on and the steamers from Belfast were packed. He took off from Ballyholme beach, flew over Groomsport, circled Bangor Bay, then came back over the heads of the spectators to land. These display flights were interspersed with trips for selected passengers. The event was rounded off on both days with a military band concert and a fireworks display.

AEROPLANE FLIGHTS FOR PASSENGERS.

Messrs. GEOFFREY SMILES, a native of Belfast ; and JOSEPH CORDNER, of Derry, both Licensed Pilots, who arrived at

PORTRUSH

BY AEROPLANE FROM LONDON,

ARE NOW TAKING PASSENGERS AT REASONABLE FARES FOR

TRIPS IN THE AIR.

To Book Flights write, phone, or wire to

"Pilots, Portrush Hotel."

An advert placed by Joe Cordner in local newspapers in 1919.
(*Guy Warner Collection*)

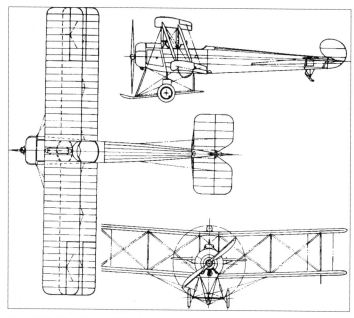

Avro 504K. (*Guy Warner Collection*)

During the course of the First World War, the aeroplane was transformed from a novelty into a practical machine capable of transporting men, fuel, bombs and guns. Thoughts turned, even while the war was still in progress, to using this lifting capacity for commercial purposes. As is still the case today, the stretch of water separating Ireland from Great Britain presented both a challenge and an opportunity. Joseph Cordner returned home in May 1919, with fellow Ulster airman, Geoffrey Smiles (RAeC Certificate No 783, 14 May 1914). Smiles was the son of the Managing Director of the Belfast Rope Works, the largest in the world at that time. He had also been an instructor at the Hall Flying School, Hendon, where Cordner had qualified for his Royal Aero Club Pilot's Certificate (No 3545, 6 September 1916). They flew a war surplus Avro 504 from London to North Antrim, crossing over from Turnberry on the Ayrshire coast, to give a series of pleasure flights around Coleraine and Ballycastle, as well as over Ballymoney, the Giant's Causeway and Bushmills. A demonstration was made of Joe Cordner's aerial bag for carrying and distributing mails, papers and parcels, when packets containing a special edition of the *Northern Constitution* were delivered on a Friday evening by air to outlying villages in the region of Ballymoney. It was thereby claimed in the newspaper that it was the first in Ireland to be distributed by air. Smiles was the brother of Sir Walter Smiles, who perished in the *Princess Victoria* disaster in 1953 and the grandson of Dr Samuel Smiles, the author of *Self-Help*.

The DH4 G-EAMU which also flew to Belfast in 1921, shown here before changing names from *City of Cardiff* to *City of York*. *(Richard Riding Collection)*

The Avro 548, G-EAPQ, which visited Belfast in 1921. *(via Anne & Brian Stanley)*

In June 1921 King George V and Queen Mary visited Northern Ireland in the Royal Yacht, to open the new parliament. Aircraft landed at Aldergrove (which had been developed as an airfield for use by the Royal Air Force as described in the first book in this series, *Military Aviation in Northern Ireland*, also by Guy Warner and Ernie Cromie) with cameramen and reporters and returned to London with newsreel films and photographs of the event. Two DH9s, both supplied for charter at a rate of two shillings (10p) a mile, through Captain DM Greig of the Air Express Company, one piloted by Alan Cobham and the other by FW Hatchett, arrived on behalf of *The Times*, *Pathé Frères* and the *Daily Graphic*. The DH4A,

G-EAMU, *City of York* of The Instone Air Line Ltd was flown in by Captain FL Barnard for the *Daily Mail* and the *Daily Mirror* and the Avro 548, G-EAPQ, with its owner, Captain EDC Herne, acting for the *Daily Sketch*, with AO Russell of Aero Films Ltd as his passenger, completed the aerial activity. Film and still photographs were taken of their Majesties' arrival at Donegal Quay and motorcade to the City Hall and rushed to the waiting aircraft, which had all departed again before 2 o'clock. *Pathé* was able to show a film of the event in London cinemas that evening, while the national newspapers included photographs of the principal parts of the ceremony the following morning.

One of the DH16s being unloaded at Aldergrove in 1922. *(Ulster Aviation Society)*

These photographs appeared in *The Times* on 6 December, plus aerial views of Belfast City Hall and of Stormont Castle.

The DH16, G-EALM, being loaded at Chester en-route to Aldergrove in 1922. *(Ulster Aviation Society)*

On 5 December 1922 a special Ulster edition of *The Times* was flown to Aldergrove from Chester in two DH16s, G-EALM and G-EAPT, of the de Havilland Aeroplane Hire Service, flown by Captain CD Barnard and HS Broad. It reviewed the economic and political developments in Northern Ireland since the establishment of the parliament. A Bristol Fighter was dispatched from Aldergrove at 11.00 am to guide the visitors and to allow a photographer from *The Times* the opportunity to take some aerial views of Belfast. At 11.30 am, the three aircraft came in sight and landed a few minutes later. The pilots commented that it been a rough passage, with the wind blowing a gale. One DH16 made the return journey before dusk the same afternoon. The other was flown to Dublin by Hubert Broad the following day and returned to England via Phoenix Park. Hubert Broad later became de Havilland's chief test pilot, while Captain Barnard became personal pilot to the Duchess of Bedford.

THE FLIGHT OF AGES

IN YE OLDEN TIME
POOR DICK WHITTINGTON
HAD TO RETURN TO LONDON
BY SHANKS MARE
BUT TO DAY :—

OUR LORD MAYOR
RETURNS TO BELFAST
BY AEROPLANE

A cartoon featuring William Turner which appeared in the *Belfast Telegraph* in October 1923. *(Belfast Central Library Newspaper Archive)*

William Turner, Alan Cobham and the DH50, G-EBFN, at Aldergrove in 1923. *(Cobham plc)*

On 15 September 1923 Alan Cobham undertook the first express airmail trial to Northern Ireland in the prototype DH50, G-EBFN. The 'dummy' service from Plymouth via Birmingham and Manchester lasted only a few weeks. The main object was the rapid conveyance of the incoming American mails, particularly those in respect of the linen trade. There was great rivalry for a share of the important American market between linen makers in the north of England, Northern Ireland and those in Northern France. It was conceived that the mail service would allow the British producers a time advantage over their competitors. A few passengers were also flown, including on 20 September, the Mayor of Plymouth, Mr Solomon Stephens and his daughter, Laura. A civic gift of Devonshire cream was brought to Belfast, in return Mr Stephens was presented with a blackthorn stick. In all, some 16 flights to Belfast were completed over a four week period. The Lord Mayor of Belfast, Alderman WS Turner (soon to be dubbed Sir William) was taken aloft by Alan Cobham for a trial flight over the city. He became an enthusiastic exponent of the potential of air transport.

DH9c, G-EBAX, at Aldergrove in 1923 with a consignment of newspapers. *(Eason & Son Ltd)*

The DH9c, G-EBAX, being unloaded at Aldergrove in 1923. *(Eason & Son Ltd)*

Newspapers were also flown from Manchester, using the DH9C, G-EBAX, during the same period, with the specially marked vans of Eason's Motor Service 'By Air To-Day', meeting the aeroplane at Aldergrove, where a ton of papers was unloaded for, 'despatch to all parts of Ulster.' It is known that these flights took place on 27, 28 and 29 September and 2 October. On one occasion at least, the pilot was Captain Walter Hope of the DH Aeroplane Hire Service. On 16 October the process was reversed, with the Belfast newspaper, the *Northern Whig* being sent to Manchester as, "the first Irish newspaper to try the experiment". Also in 1923 parachutes were dropped from an aeroplane over Balmoral from a height of 200 to 300 feet, from which were suspended a variety of items, the official report thereon stating, "Cardboard Carton – crushed due to the folding of the mail bag. Pair of spectacles in a case – undamaged. Box of chalks – undamaged. Cardboard box containing a tin of milk powder – box slightly crushed, tin intact. Cardboard box containing one stick of sealing wax – sealing wax broken. Cardboard box containing nibs, cardboard box containing crayon, cardboard box containing silver watch without glass, cardboard box containing blue refill leads and a cake of soap – all undamaged."

A photo montage on the subject of the delivery of the *Belfast Telegraph* by air in 1925. *(Belfast Telegraph)*

The opening ceremony at Malone. The Lord Mayor may be recognised by his chain of office, while, to his right, Sir Sefton Brancker is sporting a monocle. *(Cobham plc)*

As can be seen, the conditions at Malone could be muddy. *(Cobham plc)*

With the support of the Lord Mayor and the Corporation, land was purchased and an airfield established in Belfast at Malone. The first commercial flight from Malone was made by Alan Cobham on 30 April 1924 in the DH50, G-EBFP, to Liverpool, Aintree, but the sodden state of the ground that day, which rendered take-off more difficult, was a portent of the troubles facing this bold effort and the company which had been established by Donald Greig to service it, Northern Airlines. The commercial drivers of the venture were the delivery of mails and newspapers but it was also possible to carry up to four passengers. Other routes were tried – to Glasgow, Carlisle, Stranraer and Londonderry – the first internal air service in Ireland. Aircraft used were DH9s and DH50s. Sadly it came to an end just over a year after it began. It did not succeed because it was ahead of its time: it was unsubsidised, navigational and meteorological services were limited and the aircraft were relatively small with only one engine. This raised not only safety concerns but also made the carriage of economically viable loads unfeasible. The full story is told in *Flying from Malone* by Guy Warner.

The Master of Sempill visited Belfast in the DH60 Moth, G-EBKT. *(Richard Riding Collection)*

Over Christmas and the New Year 1925–26, Colonel The Master of Sempill made a record-breaking flight, which included Belfast in the route covered. Accompanied by the Director of Civil Aviation, Sir Sefton Brancker, he flew from Stag Lane in London in the prototype DH60 Moth G-EBKT. By the time he returned there he had covered the greatest distance by a light aircraft carrying a passenger within the British Isles. They landed at Aldergrove on 28 December, were entertained by Sir William Turner, and departed two days later, having been delayed by inclement weather over the whole of the British Isles. As well as Belfast, they also visited Dublin and Limerick. It is possible that this part of the trip may have encouraged the fledgling Irish Army Air Corps to purchase four Cirrus Moths in July 1926.

Short Calcutta, G-EBVH, moored in the Musgrave Channel at Belfast in 1928. *(Ulster Aviation Society)*

The Short Calcutta, G-EBVH, over the City Hall, Belfast in September 1928. *(Belfast Central Library Newspaper Archive)*

Flying boats were seen as having great potential, indeed the 1920s and 1930s may be regarded as their heyday. A trial service between Liverpool and Belfast Harbour was flown between 24 September and 4 October 1928 using the Short Calcutta G-EBVH of Imperial Airways. It was subsidised by the Corporations of the two cities. The fare in this case was £3 10s 0d (£3.50) single and £6 10s 0d (£6.50) return. The cargo on an early flight included the first delivery of Irish eggs to be sold in Liverpool on the day they were laid, of which the *Liverpool Echo* wrote, "It is possible this week for an egg to be laid in Ireland in the morning and sold in Liverpool before the stores close at 6 pm." Further evidence of growing 'airmindedness' may be seen in the formation of the North of Ireland Aero Club at the Grand Central Hotel, Belfast on 28 September 1928.

Amelia Earhart at Culmore in 1932.
(Amelia Earhart Centre)

On 22 May 1932, a very famous personality arrived at Aldergrove, the great aviatrix Amelia Earhart. The previous day, she had completed the first female solo crossing of the Atlantic from Harbour Grace, Newfoundland to a green pasture near the village of Culmore, County Londonderry in her Lockheed Vega 5B, NC7952 – a distance of 2026 miles in a time of 14 hours and 54 minutes. On landing she was greeted by a farm worker, who took her to the nearest farmhouse for a pot of tea. After travelling there by road, she departed from Aldergrove in a Desoutter air-taxi of National Flying Services and was taken onwards to London via Blackpool, to be followed by her aircraft a few days afterwards, it being taken by road to Belfast and then shipped to England.

The Lockheed Vega 5B, NC7952, flown by Amelia Earhart after landing at Culmore. *(Amelia Earhart Centre)*

The Saro Cloud, G-ABXW, which operated a brief, experimental service in 1932. *(Richard Riding Collection)*

Another experimental service was undertaken in August 1932 by British Flying Boats Ltd using the Saunders-Roe Cloud amphibian, G-ABXW, *Cloud of Iona*, in a brief operation from Greenock to Musgrave Channel, Belfast. *Aeroplane* magazine reported that on 15 August, passengers left Glasgow by car at 8.30 am for Greenock, where they were transferred by motor-boat to the waiting aeroplane, alighting in Belfast Lough at 11.30 am and were conveyed, again by motor-boat, to Queen's Bridge, "a stone's throw from the city centre". The whole journey from Greenock to Queen's Bridge, 100 miles, was covered in 55 minutes.

A visitor to Belfast in 1933, DH60 GIII Moth, G-ABZU. *(Richard Riding Collection)*

LANDING OF MASTER OF SEMPILL AT NEW AERODROME SITE, SYDENHAM. 31st MAY, 1933.

Colonel the Master of Sempill in Belfast (wearing cap). *(Belfast Harbour Commissioners)*

Sydenham before the land reclaimation began. *(Belfast Harbour Commissioners)*

Following a decade of sporadic activity, while economically practical aircraft were being developed, the Belfast Harbour Commissioners were inspired to propose a use for the new land being claimed at the mouth of the harbour on the south side of Belfast Lough at Sydenham. By May 1933, a sufficiently flat area of land, about 300 yards in diameter, was ready for the first recorded landings. On 11 May, the DH60 GIII Moth, G-ABZU, arrived at Sydenham from Renfrew, flew to Aldergrove and back and departed for Renfrew again. Then on 25 May, G-ACBZ, a DH83 Fox Moth of John Sword's Midland & Scottish Air Ferries also made the crossing from Renfrew, while on 31 May, Colonel the Master of Sempill, flying the DH80 Puss Moth G-ABJU, was another early visitor.

One of the participants in the air display at Sydenham in 1933 was the Avro 504K, G-ACCX. *(Richard Riding Collection)*

Another was the Cierva C.19, G-ABUG, shown here at Sydenham. *(Ulster Aviation Society)*

Handley Page HP.33 Clive III, G-ABYX, at Ards Airfield. *(Guy Warner Collection)*

On July 14-15, 1933 (having performed at Londonderry on 12-13), Sir Alan Cobham visited Sydenham with his National Aviation Day Display (popularly known as the Flying Circus – a name heartily disliked by Sir Alan). The aircraft participating included: DH82A Tiger Moth, G-ABUL, HP.33 Clive III, G-ABYX, Cierva Autogiros, G-ABUG and G-ABUH, DH60 Moth, G-ABUB, Spartan Three Seater II, G-ABZH, Percival Gull, G-ABUV and Avro 504K, G-ACCX. The event was well attended and promoted the new facility. The great airman was asked by the *Belfast Telegraph* for his opinion of the site. He replied, "It is a magnificent location but it is not ready yet. I have landed on it but it makes so heavy running that it is difficult to operate on it. If it had been dry it would have been excellent. There is nothing wrong with the situation but it needs to be developed. It needs town planning so to speak."

The Junkers F.13, G-ABDC, which landed in Belfast in 1933. *(Richard Riding Collection)*

A more unusual visitor on 1 September 1933 was the Junkers F.13, G-ABDC of Brooklands Airways en-route from London to Carlisle, which returned from Carlisle the following day, with half a ton (508 kg) of newspapers. On 3 September it suffered an unfortunate experience; when attempting to take-off for London, it became bogged down on the tidal mudflats in the centre of the Connswater River, slightly injuring the five passengers and sustaining minor damage. The potential of the site had therefore been explored and was judged suitable for further development. The Belfast Harbour Commissioners hired a consultant, Air Commodore JA Chamier CB, CMG, DSO, OBE and set up a management committee. In November 1935, it was decided to construct 'a large aerodrome'. Much work had to be done to bring the site up to an acceptable standard to qualify for an Air Ministry licence, particularly in respect of drainage work owing to the soggy nature of the airfield surface.

Midland & Scottish Air Ferries schedule 1933.
(Guy Warner Collection)

The Avro 618 Ten, G-ACGF, of Midland & Scottish Air Ferries. *(AJ Jackson Collection)*

Meanwhile there had been significant developments elsewhere. The first regular and sustained civil air service to and from Northern Ireland had begun on 31 May 1933 with the arrival of the Avro 618 Ten, G-ACGF, at RAF Aldergrove. The aircraft was operated by Midland & Scottish Air Ferries Ltd of Renfrew and it could accommodate up to nine passengers, on a daily service in each direction. The flights operated twice daily in the summer months, leaving Renfrew at 9.00 am and 6.00 pm, making the return journey at 10.30 am and 7.30 pm. Hired Rolls Royce or Daimler limousines provided free transport to the respective city centres. To begin with, the fares were £3.00 single and £5.00 return. A reduction to £3 10s 0d (£3.50) return was made in December 1933. Children were charged half fare. Fares from Campbeltown to Belfast were priced at £2 10s 0d (£2.50).

Sir Alan Cobham's aircraft at Aldergrove in 1933. *(Ernie Cromie Collection)*

DH84 Dragon, G-ACDL, of Midland & Scottish Air Ferries, shown here at Ronaldsway, Isle of Man. *(AJ Jackson Collection)*

Meanwhile, the first civil air display in Ulster since that held at the Balmoral Showgrounds, Belfast in 1912, took place at Aldergrove on 1 July 1933. It proved to be highly popular and included pleasure flying in the Avro Ten, G-ACGF, de Havilland Dragon, G-ACDL and DH83 Fox Moth, G-ACCT of Midland and Scottish Air Ferries. The Dragon was also used to carry out the day's scheduled services to Campbeltown and Glasgow, while the Fox Moth's first task was to collect Lord Londonderry and family. Service participation was provided by the Vickers Virginias of Aldergrove's No 502 Squadron and by Westland Wapitis from No 602 Squadron based at Renfrew. Cobham displayed in Belfast, Coleraine and Londonderry in May 1935, followed by CWA Scott in 1936 at Lurgan, Broughshane, Ards, Coleraine, Derry and Omagh.

Seen here at Speke, Liverpool, the DH89 Dragon Rapide, G-ADAL, of Hillman's Airways, probably on the inaugural London – Belfast – Glasgow mail flight on 1 December 1934. *(via John Stroud)*

The Airspeed Ferry, G-ACFB, of Midland and Scottish Air Ferries. *(AJ Jackson Collection)*

The next major development for Aldergrove was on 27 March 1934 with the establishment of a Liverpool–Isle of Man–Belfast service which would use not only the Dragon and Avro Ten aircraft but also the Airspeed Ferrys, G-ACBT and G-ACFB. Sadly it was the end of the line for John Sword who was 'encouraged' to return to his original business of motor transport, with the final Midland & Scottish schedules being flown to Aldergrove in July. Following its demise, the Midland & Scottish (M&S) GPO mail contract for the London (now based at the 'Essex Air Port' Stapleford)–Liverpool –Belfast route was taken over by Hillman's Airways on 16 July 1934. Previously Hillman's had worked in partnership with M&S with a connection from Liverpool to Romford. Several of the M&S pilots were taken on by Edward Hillman. Soon it was running in parallel with a schedule operated by Railway Air Services (RAS), which was owned by the four main railway companies and Imperial Airways.

A Railway Air Services notice of 1934. *(Clive Moore Collection)*

The Railway Air Services DH86, G-ACVY, *Mercury. (Ernie Cromie Collection)*

Railway Air Services Timetable. *(Clive Moore Collection)*

The comfortable passenger cabin of a DH86. *(via John Stroud)*

The first RAS schedule between Croydon (London), Castle Bromwich (Birmingham), Barton (Manchester), Aldergrove and Renfrew (Glasgow) was flown by the DH86s, G-ACVY *Mercury* and G-ACPL *Delphinus* on 20 August 1934. Liverpool was added to the schedule from 15 April 1935. Typical return fares, which covered the cost of road transport to/from the centre of Belfast were, London £9, Liverpool £4 10s 0d (£4.50) and Glasgow £3 5s 0d (£3.25). Flying time to Liverpool was 1 hour 15 minutes, with London being reached after about another hour in the air.

Lady Londonderry christening her husband's Avro Cadet, Finnian the White, at the official opening of Ards Airport. *(Ernie Cromie Collection)*

Guests at the opening of Ards Airport, the Londonderry family is on the right of the picture. *(Ernie Cromie Collection)*

A new, purpose built civil aerodrome was officially opened on 31 August 1934 by the Duke of Abercorn, the Governor of Northern Ireland, the 'Ards Airport', at Newtownards. Its establishment owed much to the 7th Marquis of Londonderry, who made 50 acres of his estate adjoining the Comber Road available and was closely involved in the plans for the airport. The first officially recorded landing had taken place at the end of June, The aircraft was a de Havilland Gipsy Moth and the pilot was a Scotsman, Fred McNeill. On 31 July a Hillman's airliner landed at the airfield. On board were Ladies Margaret, Helen and Mairi Stewart who had flown from London to stay in their home at Mount Stewart. The management of the airfield was leased to Airwork Limited of Heston. Lord Londonderry, who was Secretary of State for Air from 1931–1935, was himself an enthusiastic and able pilot – keeping two aircraft at Newtownards, an Avro 638 Cadet, G-ACTX and a GA Monospar ST-4, G-AEPG. He later owned a Percival Q.6, G-AFHG and also built a small hangar adjacent to his private airstrip at Mount Stewart. His daughter, Lady Mairi, owned a DH87 Hornet Moth, G-ADMR. He also set up a flying school and appointed Flight Lieutenant RWE Bryant as Chief Instructor and Manager. The North of Ireland Flying Club, which had been formed in 1928, was also offered a home at the new aerodrome. The airfield was twice a checkpoint in the famous King's Cup Air Race in 1935 and 1937.

Mail being unloaded from the Hillman's Airways
DH89 Dragon Rapide, G-ADAG, at Ards in 1935.
(North of Ireland Philatelic Society)

An aerial view of Ards Airport prior to its wartime redevelopment. *(E Cromie Collection)*

Air Traffic Control at Ards in the 1930s.
(via Tommy Maddock)

Spartan II Cruiser, G-ACZM, at Ards. *(Ernie Cromie Collection)*

Commercial services were gradually transferred to Ards from Aldergrove, beginning with the Hillman's operation and thus ended the first phase of its life as a civil airport on 23 May 1936, when RAS moved to Ards. Before the transfer, DH89 Rapides had been introduced as back-up aircraft to the DH86s. Interestingly, before the demise of Midland and Scottish, John Sword had conducted negotiations with the Belfast Corporation regarding the feasibility of using the Malone site again, as he was aware that the Air Ministry was keen for Aldergrove to revert to purely military use. These came to nothing chiefly because Malone's drainage problems would have required considerable expenditure to solve.

Von Ribbentrop's Ju52 at Ards.
(Ernie Cromie Collection)

DH89 Dragon Rapide, G-ADDF, of Northern & Scottish Airways Ltd at Ards. *(Guy Warner Collection)*

Services to Ards were provided by Hillman's Airways and United Airways, which were merged into British Airways in 1936, which resulted in their connections to Glasgow, Blackpool, the Isle of Man and Liverpool being passed over to George Nicholson's Northern and Scottish Airways, which was affiliated to the same group, all controlled by Whitehall Securities. During 1936 Ards handled some 6000 passengers. One of these arrivals was a Junkers Ju52 bringing the German Ambassador, Joachim Von Ribbentrop, on a private visit to Mount Stewart in May.

Mail being unloaded from the Railway Air Services DH86, G-AEFH, *Neptune*, at Ards. *(Ernie Cromie Collection)*

Ards Airport with the famous Scrabo tower in the background. *(Tommy Maddock Collection)*

In a further re-organisation of domestic air services in May 1937, the routes again changed hands, passing to Railway Air Services and its associate company the Manx Airway, which was formed by the Isle of Man Steam Packet Co and the LMS Railway. All civil flights were now concentrated at Ards. For a time between 1935 and 1937 competition to Blackpool and the Isle of Man was offered by Blackpool and West Coast Air Services (which became simply West Coast Air Services in 1937). During the same year Isle of Man Air Services (IoMAS) took over and also assimilated the Manx Airway, thus putting all business in the hands of RAS and IoMAS, which was a 'Railway Associated Airline'. By 1938 the volume of traffic was such that Ards was placed seventh in the list of Airports for the British Isles handling 2075 aircraft, with 3269 passenger arrivals and 2889 departing. It also handled 21 tons of mail and it was second only to Croydon in terms of other freight services.

An aerial view of the Opening Day at Belfast Harbour Airport. *(Belfast Harbour Commissioners)*

What Belfast Harbour Airport would have looked like, had the war not halted progress. The hangars on the left were those built by Opening Day. *(Belfast Harbour Commissioners)*

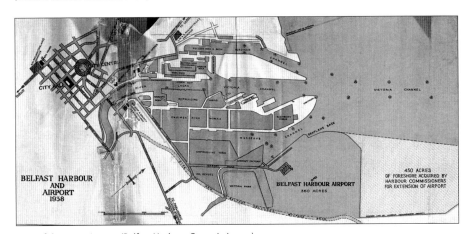

Map of the new airport. *(Belfast Harbour Commissioners)*

Belfast Harbour Airport was opened by Mrs Neville Chamberlain. *(Belfast Harbour Commissioners)*

On 11 September 1937, Notice to Airmen No 197 issued by the Air Ministry confirmed the issue of a public-use licence for Belfast Aerodrome, Sydenham. On 16 March 1938 Mrs Neville Chamberlain, the wife of the Prime Minister, officially opened Belfast Harbour Airport. The opening ceremony was considered of sufficient importance to be broadcast nationally on radio by the BBC. Commercial flying was transferred from Ards and, that afternoon, a DH86 Express of Railway Air Services departed for Glasgow on the inaugural flight, followed by a Ronaldsway-bound DH89 Rapide of Isle of Man Air Services.

BELFAST TELEGRAPH, MONDAY, JULY 4, 1938.

SEEN BY HUNDREDS
Destruction Of A 'Plane

AIR LINER CRASHES

IN MARSHY FIELD NEAR BELFAST

AND BURSTS INTO FLAMES

PILOT AND ENGINEER DEAD

NO PASSENGERS ON BOARD

Before the horrified gaze of hundreds of people strolling near Belfast on Sunday evening, a Railway Air Services passenger aeroplane arriving at the Harbour Airport from Glasgow crashed in a marshy field near Tillysburn, on the Holywood Road, and burst into flames.

THE TWO OCCUPANTS, THE PILOT AND ENGINEER, WERE KILLED INSTANTLY. THERE WERE NO PASSENGERS ON BOARD. THE DEAD MEN ARE:—

CAPTAIN A. C. LARMUTH, OF LONDON, THE PILOT; AND
REGINALD VAUGHAN, OF LONDON, THE ENGINEER AND OBSERVER.

"STAR OF SCOTIA."

The burnt-out wreckage of the 'plane, a two-engined machine named "Star of Scotia," is being examined by experts from Railway Air Services and the Air Ministry in order to find the cause of the crash, which so far has not been established.

According to Mr. Lewis Dunn, of Demense Road, Holywood, who was the first to reach the machine after the crash, it was approaching the airport at a height of 300 feet when it nose-dived to the ground.

PULLED OUT LARMUTH.

At great personal risk Mr. Dunn and Mr. Thomas Corkill, of Strandburn Avenue, Belfast, pulled the body of Captain Larmuth from the burning wreckage.

His Last Day on Service

TO-DAY Captain Larmuth, pilot of the ill-fated "Star of Scotia," was to have taken up duty as an instructor at a flying school at Prestwick, Ayrshire.

His fiancee lives in Glasgow.

Captain Larmuth was an experienced pilot who had been on the London-Belfast-Glasgow service for many years.

Reginald Vaughan, the engineer, was aged 33 and was married a year ago at Gretna Green.

Larmuth had been taken to the Royal Victoria Hospital, where it was established that death must have taken place instantaneously. He had received multiple injuries. It is thought that Mr. Vaughan was also dead before the flames enveloped the wreck.

HOLYWOOD ROAD THRONGED.

The Holywood road was thronged with Sunday evening sightseers, who watched the plane as it prepared to land. Within a few moments of the crash the burning pieces of metal was circled by a crowd, which the police, under District-Inspector Geelan and Head-Constable Leyburn, eventually dispersed. Some of the crowd took possession of pieces of the scattered wreckage.

Officials of the Harbour Airport and Railway Air Services then arrived and the wreckage was placed under official surveillance. By Air Ministry regulations a police guard must be placed over any aircraft which crashes until examination by experts. To-day the twisted and blackened framework, all that remains of the glistening silver "Star of Scotia," is watched over by the police.

Some light on the tragedy may be given by the logbook and altimeter which are stated to have been recovered. The coloured flag of the machine was also picked up.

A mystery of the crash was the discovery of a Verey light pistol fully loaded which, according to a witness, was in Captain Larmuth's hand when he attempted to get clear as the machine fell.

Official Statement

THE following official statement has been issued:—

"Railway Air Services, Ltd., regret to announce that one of their 'planes when landing at Belfast on Sunday evening crashed close to the airport.

"There were no passengers in the 'plane, but unfortunately the pilot, Captain Larmuth, and Engineer Vaughan were killed."

Report of the crash in the *Belfast Telegraph* the following day.
(Belfast Central Library Newspaper Archive)

DH89, G-AEBX at Ronaldsway Airport, Isle of Man in 1936. *(Terry Faragher)*

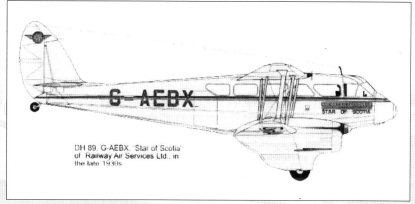

DH89, G-AEBX, *Star of Scotia. (Scale Aircraft Modeller)*

Tragically, on 3 July 1938 RAS DH89, G-AEBX, *Star Of Scotia* crashed near Tillysburn on approach to Belfast from Renfrew, the two crew members being killed, Acting Captain AC Larmuth and engineer, Reginald Vaughan. According to eye-witnesses the Rapide was making a normal descent when the engines stopped, it went into a left hand spin and struck the ground with great force, bursting into flames. Two members of the public rushed to the scene and dragged the pilot from the wreckage but the fire was burning too fiercely to attempt to save the engineer. To their horror, seven waiting passengers at the airport witnessed the crash of the aircraft on which they had been going to fly to Glasgow.

DH86, G-AEFH, *Neptune* of Railway Air Services taking off from Belfast Harbour Airport. *(via John Stroud)*

DH86A, G-ACZP, in its wartime livery at Speke. *(via John Stroud)*

Belfast Harbour Airport operated restricted civil schedules during the war. A limited service was maintained under the auspices of the Allied Airways Joint Committee based at Liverpool. DH89 Rapides, with cabin windows painted white for security purposes, connected Belfast Harbour Airport with Liverpool from March 1940 and Glasgow from May 1940 onwards. With victory in Europe coming closer an important new connection was made. On 13 November 1944 an extended Croydon–Liverpool–Belfast service was inaugurated by the RAS DH86A, G-ACZP. The fare was £8.00 single and £13.00 return.

An Avro Nineteen of Railway Air Services at Speke Airport, Liverpool. *(via Bert Hutchinson)*

The Avro Nineteen's rather ulititarian interior. *(via John Stroud)*

Railway Air Services Avro Nineteen, G-AGUE on the ground at Dublin Airport. *(via John Stroud)*

A year later on 3 December 1945 an Avro Nineteen of RAS inaugurated the first non-stop Sydenham to Croydon service, in a time of 2 hours and 20 minutes, carrying six passengers and flown by Captain AL Freeman. This aircraft was a development of the famous Anson and could carry six to nine passengers. It was very much a stopgap interim type and had been produced to meet the requirements of the Brabazon Committee Specification XIX for a feeder liner.

The DH89A, G-AERN, of West Coast Air Services. *(via John Stroud)*

C-47A Dakota G-AGZA, taking off from Renfrew for Belfast. *(via John Stroud)*

Railway Air Services DH89A, G-AERZ, which crashed at Craigavad in 1946. *(via John Stroud)*

With the coming of peace, Railway Air Services, the dominant pre-war domestic carrier, lost no time in setting up a base at Belfast Harbour Airport, Sydenham for services to London, Liverpool and (from 1946) Manchester. The initial London–Belfast–Manchester schedule was flown on 29 July, by the RAS Avro Nineteen, G-AHIB. The Glasgow schedule was operated for RAS by Scottish Airways (formed in 1937 from the amalgamation of Northern and Scottish Airways with Highland Airways), who introduced the 20 passenger C-47A Dakota, when flying G-AGZA from Renfrew to Belfast on 13 May 1946. West Coast Air Services flew on behalf of RAS from Liverpool, with the DH86B, G-ADYH and the DH89A, G-AERN. The Isle of Man and Prestwick were also served by Isle of Man Air Services and Scottish Airlines respectively. The route from Prestwick was inaugurated on 28 January 1946 with the Dakota, G-AGWS. The year was marred by a tragedy on 1 April, when the RAS DH89A, G-AERZ, flying from Liverpool, crashed on the golf course at Craigavad on approach to Belfast in fog. The crew of two and six passengers were killed.

Lord Nathan, Minister of Civil Aviation, inspecting Nutts Corner with Mr W Kearney, airport manager. *(PRONI D2334/4/3/22)*

Nutts Corner Control Tower.
(Belfast Telegraph)

One of the consequences of the wartime airfield construction programme was the building of Nutts Corner, just three miles from Aldergrove. Because the air base had been developed with large RAF Coastal Command and USAAF aircraft in mind, there were relatively long runways (6000, 4800 and 3700 feet in length) and concrete parking aprons available for the bigger commercial aircraft which were anticipated. Therefore on 1 December 1946, Nutts Corner replaced Belfast Harbour as Northern Ireland's civil airport. On a Sunday morning, just before Christmas, a DH89,

Avro Nineteen and a Ju52 left Belfast Harbour Airport for Nutts Corner, laden with all the office equipment, desks, chairs and files. Civil flying from Sydenham continued on a more limited basis, including in 1948, Rochester Air Charter Service, owned by Shorts, which offered passenger and freight flights, including local flights to Bangor and back for 10/- (50p). It had a variety of aircraft including two DH Rapides, an Avro Nineteen, two Percival Proctors, a DH Dragonfly, two Tiger Moths, an Auster I and a Miles Magister.

Junkers Ju52, G-AHOF, at Nutts Corner. *(via John Stroud)*

The Fokker F.XXII, G-AFZP, of Scottish Airlines. *(Richard Riding Collection)*

In 1946, the Labour Government established the British European Airways Corporation as a state-owned airline, with a monopoly of scheduled air services within the United Kingdom. Initially, the Corporation's services between London and Belfast were operated by Railway Air Services, the first non-stop service by BEA from Croydon to Nutts Corner being on 20 March 1947, by the Junkers Ju52/3m, G-AHOF, one of a fleet of these veteran tri-motors taken from Germany as war reparations and used briefly without conspicuous success. (Ju52s had been operating on the Croydon–Liverpool–Belfast route since November 1946, with the first service on the 18th by RAS Ju52/3m G-AHOG, which was painted in BEA colours.) Another very unusual type which was used between December 1946 and August 1947 by Scottish Airlines from Prestwick was the four-engine, high winged, 22 seat, 1935 vintage Fokker F.XXII, G-AFZP, a former KLM aircraft which had escaped to England from the German invasion of Holland during the war. It must have made quite a sight in the orange and silver livery of the airline, which flew the service under contract to BEA.

Aer Lingus DC-3 being refuelled at Dublin in the late 1940s. *(Aer Rianta)*

The nose section of the graceful SE.161 Languedoc. *(Guy Warner Collection)*

The Aer Lingus DC-3, EI-AFC, at Nutts Corner. *(Bert McGowan)*

With the end of the Second World War, Aer Lingus planned an ambitious expansion of its network and services, and it was envisaged that Belfast would play a key role in this development. In mid-January 1947 Aer Lingus officials carried out an inspection of Nutts Corner Airport to review the facilities and make preliminary arrangements for the start of operations there later in the year. It was planned to open an Aer Lingus branch office in Belfast to handle passengers travelling on its services to Dublin and to the planned new destinations in the UK, as well as bookings for a transatlantic service. 1 August 1947 saw the start of the first Dublin–Belfast service, followed by Dublin–Belfast–Liverpool on 6 October 1947,

with DC-3 aircraft. It soon became clear that traffic expectations on many of the newly-launched routes were overly optimistic and with losses starting to mount rapidly, the Belfast services were terminated in January 1948. Another relatively short-lived service was flown by Air France. On 13 June 1949 it began a direct link between Nutts Corner and Paris, Le Bourget, using 33-seat, four-engined SE.161 Languedoc airliners. It operated three days per week, on Mondays, Wednesdays and Saturdays from Belfast, taking three hours with a return fare of £28 16s 0d, with a cheaper rate at the weekend and provided a summer schedule in 1949 and 1950.

BEA's inaugural DC-3 flight to Nutts Corner 19 May 1947. *(Guy Warner Collection)*

NUTT'S CORNER AIRPORT, BELFAST

Two BEA Dakotas in front of the spectators' terrace at Nutts Corner. *(Jim Rankin)*

On 19 May 1947, DC-3 Dakotas replaced the Ju52s and the London terminal changed to Northolt. Some of the early routes, which in 1947 included Liverpool, Manchester, the Isle of Man, Glasgow, Carlisle and Newcastle, were flown by BEA using the long-serving DH Rapides, as well as Avro Nineteens. Carlisle and Newcastle lasted only a few months as destinations, while Birmingham was added to the route structure in May 1950.

Dan-Air Avro York, G-ANTJ, at Nutts Corner.
(Bert McGowan)

Avro Lancastrian G-AHBZ. *(via Peter Myers)*

During September and October 1947 and again in the autumn of 1948, a considerable civil air operation took place. Because of severe milk shortages in England, which was matched by a surplus in Northern Ireland, an airlift from Nutts Corner to Speke Airport in Liverpool and Squire's Gate, Blackpool was organised. The advantage over using sea transport was that the milk would arrive fresh and not sour. The milk was carried in 10-gallon churns by a variety of charter companies using Avro Yorks and Lancastrians, Handley Page Halifaxes and Haltons, Douglas Dakotas, Consolidated Liberators and Miles Aerovans. A York could carry between 1450 and 1500 gallons, while a Lancastrian could take 950 to 1000 gallons. On 3 October 1947 one of the milk carriers came to grief, fortunately without any loss of life. It was a very foggy morning when the Avro Lancastrian 3, G-AHBU, *Sky Path* of Skyways Ltd attempted to take-off with a full load of 1000 gallons of milk in churns. It failed to gain height and tore through a boundary fence before disintegrating and burning out. The pilot, navigator and

radio officer were saved by Skyways' milk loaders and airport crash crew, who had rushed to the scene. Sadly, the following year, a fatal accident occurred. A Halifax C.VIII, G-AJNZ, of World Air Freight Ltd departed Nutts Corner on the morning of 28 September 1948 carrying 1140 gallons of milk. It crashed into high ground on the Isle of Man, with the loss of all four crew members. At its peak the Ulster Milk Lift resulted in up to 30,000 gallons of milk a day being transported by air. The cost to the consumer was subsidised by the government by about two or three pence a pint. There is no doubt that some of the skills learned on this operation were soon applied in the more testing circumstances of the Berlin Airlift. Retired Air Traffic Controller, Bill Eames, recalls that a Non Directional Beacon was set up on Mew Island to assist the flow of traffic on a 24 hour basis. Furthermore a 'Baltic Exchange' was established in a hut at Nutts Corner to allocate jobs to aircrew and aircraft.

Rt Hon Anthony Eden MP, with Lord Londonderry at Ards Airport.
(PRONI D2334/4/3/37)

This photograph was taken in 1947 at Ards, it shows a Ford Prefect being loaded for the first car-carrying flight to the Isle of Man in the Miles Aerovan, G-AJTD. Mr RE Hamilton, Main Ford Dealer, appears in the photograph with Wing Commander TWT McComb OBE, Managing Director of Ulster Aviation. The car had been sold to an antique dealer on the Isle of Man.
(Ernie Cromie Collection)

Miles Aerovans were operated by Ulster Aviation Ltd (formed as Londonderry Air Charter in November 1946 by Lord Londonderry) and had a fleet of six of these boxy transports at Newtownards, including the Mk.2 G-AGWO and the Mk.4s G-AJKJ, 'KU, 'OB, 'TD and 'HD. They were employed from 1947–1949 on tourist traffic to the Isle of Man and Blackpool. Freight was charged at three shillings (15p) per ton mile. A return trip from Newtownards to the Isle of Man for a party of nine passengers would have cost 37 shillings (£1.85) per head, while the return fare to Blackpool was £4. No less than four Aerovans were lost in accidents between 1947 and 1948, G-AGWO, G-AJOB, G-AJKJ and G-AJTD, thankfully without serious injury to anyone. The tail-boom of 'TD was used as a mast for a windsock mounted on top of an old aerodrome defence pill-box for many years. In the summer of 1948 the company was granted a BEA Associate Agreement for regular tourist flights between Newtownards and Aberdeen. Ulster Aviation also operated an Airspeed Consul G-AIKT, a pair of Rapides G-AGIF and G-AHLN, a Miles Falcon Six G-AECC, Miles Gemini Mk1As G-AIHM and G-AKEJ and finally, two Miles Messenger Mk.2As, G-AJFH and 'KL. On 26 February 1949, Ulster Aviation and Mannin Airways established North-West Airlines (IOM) as a joint venture, with Rapides and the Aerovan G-AJKU, as well as several Geminis and Messengers. In 1950–1951 the company operated a scheduled service between Belfast, Blackpool and Leeds but was bought out by the Lancashire Aircraft Corporation which was based at Blackpool.

Top: Security was much more relaxed at airports in the 1950s, as this view of BEA DC-3 Pionair, G-AGHS, taken at Nutts Corner shows. *(Ernie Cromie Collection)*

Centre: Vickers Viking 1A, G-AHOP. *(Richard Riding Collection)*

Bottom: BEA's elegant Elizabethan Class brought new levels of comfort on the Belfast to London route. *(Guy Warner Collection)*

Mr HP Finch, Nutts Corner Airport Commandant with a DH Dove in the background. *(PRONI D2334/2/9/66)*

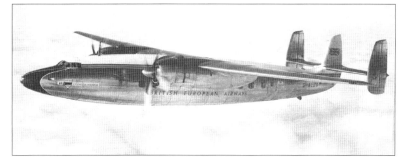

On 19 August 1949 a BEA DC-3, G-AHCY, took off from Nutts Corner for Manchester. It crashed into the side of a mist-covered hill some 15 miles from Ringway Airport, 24 of the 32 passengers and crew lost their lives. Throughout the 1950s, Nutts Corner handled nearly all of Northern Ireland's airline traffic. BEA successively used DC-3s (named the *Pionair* class after being converted by Scottish Aviation at Prestwick to 32 passenger configuration and with built-in airstairs), Vickers Vikings (a tubby 36-seater based on the Wellington bomber and named the *Admiral* class) from 1951 and Airspeed Ambassadors from 1953 to destinations in England, Scotland and the Isle of Man. A very elegant looking aircraft, the Ambassador had the BEA class name *Elizabethan*. It was the largest piston-engine aircraft ever operated by BEA. Power was supplied by two Bristol Centaurus radial piston engines and the aircraft cruised at 240 mph. *Admiral* and *Pionair* class aircraft continued to fly the Northolt route until October 1954.

Bill Eames, in the centre, was the talkdown air traffic controller on 5 January 1953.
(*Ernie Cromie Collection*)

The ill-fated Vickers Viking 1B, G-AJDL.
(*Richard Riding Collection*)

On 5 January 1953, the BEA Viking 1B, G-AJDL, *Lord St Vincent*, departed from Northolt at 7.27 pm, on the BE556 service, arriving over Nutts Corner some two hours later. When the aircraft was three miles (4.8 km) out from the runway threshold, it was 90 feet (27 m) above the glideslope. It then descended rapidly and hit approach lights a short distance from the runway, then a mobile standard beam approach van and finally the Instrument Landing System building about 200 yards from the runway, before breaking up, with the loss of 27 lives. There were eight survivors: the steward and seven passengers. This was the worst single air disaster to occur in Northern Ireland. A Board of Enquiry, chaired by Sir David Scott Cairns QC, concluded that the pilot, Captain Hartley, made "errors of judgement" but that no moral blame was to be attached to him regarding the accident. On the 60th Anniversary of the crash, the Ulster Aviation Society and Antrim Borough Council combined to stage a commemorative event which gave closure to relatives of the victims and also to surviving members of staff who had assisted with the recovery and rescue effort.

BOAC Lockheed Constellation, G-AKCE, photographed at London Airport on 12 September 1954. (Alan Scholefield)

Just before midnight on Sunday 22 March 1953, BOAC Constellation G-AKCE departed Nutts Corner on a scheduled commercial flight. Twenty-four of the passengers on board were rugby players and officials from Queen's University who were travelling to the USA. The flight originated in London and arrived at Nutts Corner from Prestwick, the intention being that it would fly on to New York via Gander. However, weather conditions caused a delay at Prestwick and, in turn, after 'CE left Nutts Corner, it required to refuel at Shannon before going on to New York. The return trip to Nutts Corner was scheduled for Tuesday 28 April but the aircraft developed engine problems over the Atlantic which required it to divert to London, with the result that the rugby team returned to Nutts Corner on Wednesday, on another BOAC Constellation en route to New York. It is believed that this was the first planned trans-Atlantic flight from/to Nutts Corner. Previously, Nutts Corner had seen a couple of Constellations but they were scheduled flights between other airports which had been required to divert because of unanticipated problems. It did not develop into a regular BOAC service.

Loading mail on to a BEA Viscount at Nutts Corner in 1961. *(North of Ireland Philatelic Society)*

BEA *Ambassador* and *Viscount*. *(Guy Warner Collection)*

Ulster Flyer Advert.

BEA Viscount and DC-3 G-AIWD seen from the terrace at Nutts Corner in 1955. *(Ernie Cromie Collection)*

On 1 November 1953 BEA introduced the *Ulster Flyer* all-first-class service from Belfast to London Airport, Heathrow – the first turbo-prop service on the route – by Vickers Viscount G-AMOD. The Viscount's flight time was 1 hour and 35 minutes; the *Elizabethan's* was 1 hour 40 minutes. (Viscounts were also used on mixed class services while *Elizabethans* also operated the *Ulster Flyer*). The *Ulster Flyer* lasted until 1960. In 1956, Jersey–Belfast was added to the BEA route structure, using *Pionairs*.

DC-3, G-AMVC, of BKS Air Transport Ltd. *(Richard Riding Collection)*

BKS advert. *(Belfast Central Library Newspaper Archive)*

Cambrian Airways DH Heron, G-ANCI. *(Richard Riding Collection)*

Silver City Heron, G-AOZN. *(Richard Riding Collection)*

Hunting Clan maintained a service from Newcastle with DC-3s in the mid-1950s and then BKS Air Transport provided services to Leeds/Bradford starting on 15 May 1955, Edinburgh in 1956 and Newcastle from 23 May 1958, using Dakotas to begin with and then also Ambassadors from 1957. In May 1956, Cambrian

Airways began operating from Cardiff and Bristol to Belfast, with the 17-passenger 4-engine DH Heron 2, G-AOGU, flying the first service, until in 1958 the service was suspended when the company experienced financial difficulties. Silver City Airways flew from Blackpool, using DH Herons, DC-3s and Bristol Freighters.

To Scotland in 17 minutes
by the
SILVER CITY AIR FERRY
* * *
Frequent daily services, including Sundays,
for cars, cycles and passengers from Belfast
(Newtownards Airport) to Stranraer (Castle
Kennedy Airport). Available for passengers
not accompanying vehicles.

Silver City also operate all-the-year-round
services to the Continent and Guernsey.

* * *

Full particulars from your Travel Agent
or
SILVER CITY AIRWAYS LTD.
Newtownards Airport, Newtownards, Co. Down
Telephone : Newtownards 2320
or
THE GENERAL STEAM NAVIGATION CO. LTD.
95 Bothwell Street, Glasgow, C.2
Telephone : Central 6643

Bristol Freighter at Ards.
(Peter Duff)

A Jaguar D-Type sports car drives off the Silver City Bristol Freighter, G-AGVC, at Ards.
(Tommy Maddock)

Silver City also used the capacious Bristol from 1955 to 1957 on a car ferry service between Castle Kennedy (near Stranraer) and Newtownards (also flying from the Harbour Airport for a few months in 1956 while the runway at Ards was extended). Flights to RAF Woodvale and the Isle of Man were also offered from Ards briefly during 1955–1956. There were four rotations daily between Ards and Castle Kennedy, the scheduled flight time was only 17 minutes. Cars cost from £7 to £7 10s 0d (£7.50), depending upon length, motorcycles from £1 to £3 for combinations, passengers were £2 10s 0d (£2.50) with children under 12 half fare and bicycles 2s 6d (13p). The initial schedule commenced on 7 April. Unfortunately the route did not prove to be as profitable as the company had hoped; there were simply not enough tourists. Some capacity was taken up with the delivery of new cars to Northern Ireland and of carpets from Cyril Lord's factories in the other direction.

Viscount G-AOHN at Nutts Corner on 13 April 1959. *(via Joe Brown)*

BEA Vickers Viscount, G-AOJA. *(Richard Riding Collection)*

In 1957 the first of the larger Viscount 800 series began operating with BEA from Nutts Corner to Heathrow. This was configured for 16 first class and 42 economy passengers and could cruise at 325 mph. By this time the whole schedule was operated by Viscounts. On the afternoon of 23 October 1957 BEA Viscount, G-AOJA on a non-scheduled, positioning flight from London, crashed at Nutts Corner when overshooting following a radar approach in bad weather with the loss of all on board, five crew and two passengers. No official cause of the crash could be determined by the subsequent Public Enquiry. There was some evidence to suggest that the airport's approach lighting may have been switched off at the time of the Viscount's landing attempt but this could not be proven. A bent screwdriver was found in the wreckage but was removed before its position in the wreckage could be determined and the likelihood of it jamming the flight controls could not be assessed. Eighteen months later, the 57 passengers and five crew on board Viscount G-AOHN were more fortunate, all escaping serious injury. The aircraft, on the early afternoon flight from London on 13 April 1959, was landing on a wet Runway 28 in a cross-wind of 25–30 knots when it ran off the side on to soft ground and the nose-wheel collapsed.

An aerial view of Nutts Corner in 1961. *(via John Stroud)*

The control tower and passenger terminal at Nutts Corner. *(Belfast Telegraph)*

In 1960 Nutts Corner was nearing the end of its days as Northern Ireland's main civil airport; BEA, with its Viscounts held sway on the main trunk routes to London Heathrow, Manchester, Birmingham and Glasgow, whilst also offering flights to the Isle of Man, Liverpool and summer service to Jersey. Cambrian Airways provided flights to Cardiff and Bristol, using the smaller Vickers Viscount 700 series. BKS Air Transport flew to Leeds/Bradford, Newcastle, Dublin and Edinburgh, using Airspeed Ambassadors and Douglas DC-3s. Silver City Airways flew DC-3s to Blackpool and the Isle of Man.

A busy scene at Nutts Corner with BEA Viscounts and Vanguard.
(Bert McGowan)

A very rare colour image of the
control tower at Nutts Corner.
(Ernie Cromie Collection)

This BEA de Havilland Comet flew the regular
schedule from London to Nutts Corner on
3 August 1961 as there were no Vanguards
serviceable. *(PRONI D2334/7/1/44)*

1961 brought the first BEA Vickers Vanguard service from Nutts Corner to Heathrow. The 'double bubble' fuselage Vanguard had a capacity for 139 passengers and several tonnes of freight. It was powered by four Rolls Royce Tyne turboprops and cruised at 400 mph. This was a type that was well-loved and admired by aircrew, ground staff, engineers and passengers alike, and served the route to London for the next 12 years.

Far left: Derby Airways DC-3, G-AOFZ. *(Tim Walden)*

Left: Cambrian Airways DC-3, G-AGHM. *(Tommy Maddock)*

A pair of Aer Lingus Fokker F.27 Friendships at Dublin Airport on 20 September 1965. *(Matthew McGrath)*

For Christmas 1960, Aer Lingus introduced a series of Dublin–Belfast flights which were geared towards providing connections to the transatlantic service from Dublin. These flights operated on 19, 22, 23 and 24 December, and they were sufficiently successful to enable a service to be introduced in the following year. On 30 April 1961 Aer Lingus resumed scheduled Dublin–Belfast flights with Fokker F.27 Friendships. In order to minimise costs, Belfast was an en-route stop between Glasgow and Dublin. This lasted until 1981, with Shannon being added in 1967. In April 1962 Derby Airways, which used DC-3s, commenced flying to Nutts Corner from the old

Derby Airport at Burnaston. In the same year Silver City Airways was absorbed by the British United Airways group and from that time BU (CI) Airways and BU (Manx) Airways provided services to Blackpool, Exeter, Bournemouth and the Isle of Man respectively, using DC-3s and Handley Page Dart Heralds. Cambrian Airways took over the flights to the Isle of Man and Liverpool from BEA in spring 1963. The Herald also made its first appearance in BEA service at Nutts Corner on 29 March 1963 when G-APWB replaced the normal Viscount on the run from Glasgow.

A DC-4 of Indian carrier Bharat Airways at a rain-swept Nutts Corner.
(Brian Finch)

A Super Constellation of the Flying Tiger Line at Nutts Corner in early 1963.
(Guy Warner Collection)

DC-6B PH-DFA of KLM at Nutts Corner. *(Brian Finch)*

The largest aircraft to land at Nutts Corner was this C-74 Douglas Globemaster in 1963. *(Joe Brown)*

International traffic from Nutts Corner, which began in the late 1950s, was all charter work, with Boeing Stratocruisers and Constellations of BOAC, Douglas DC-4s of the Flying Tiger Line and KLM, Douglas DC-6s in the livery of Pan Am and Capitol Airways, Lockheed Super Constellations of Seaboard and Western Airlines and Bristol Britannias of Canadian Pacific gracing the local skies.

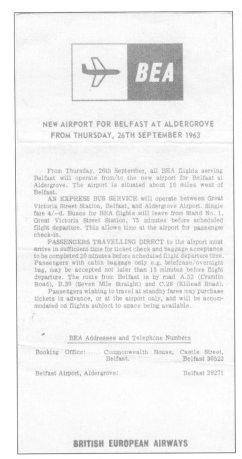

This is a very rare piece of documentary evidence of the move from Nutts Corner to Aldergrove.
(Clive Moore Collection)

Today, the former airport terminal area is the site of a motor racing circuit, a Sunday market and a supermarket distribution depot. *(Ernie Cromie Collection)*

Pan Am DC-6 at Nutts Corner with the Belfast Girls Choir.
(via Adrian Hanna)

Once again, the ever increasing size of passenger aircraft and the prospect of transatlantic travel meant that an existing site came to be considered as having had its day. Moreover, even though it was just a few miles away, Aldergrove had less variable weather conditions than those at Nutts Corner. It had been a regular diversion airfield when Nutts Corner was fog-bound. So the wheel turned full circle and 42 years after first receiving civil flights, Aldergrove became the civil airport for the Province in September 1963. The decision to restore civil aviation to Aldergrove had been made on 29 July 1959.

Queen Elizabeth, the Queen Mother visits the BEA desk during the official opening in October 1963. *(via Tony Moore)*

Model of Belfast Airport, February 1963. *(PRONI D2334/1/5/15)*

The exterior of the passenger terminal at Aldergrove in the autumn of 1963. *(Ernie Cromie Collection)*

On 26 September 1963, operations transferred to Aldergrove, which therefore became the civil airport for Northern Ireland, while remaining a major RAF station. The first scheduled commercial flight that day was an incoming BEA Viscount from Manchester, which landed at 00.23, followed by a Vanguard, G-APEH, from London. The previous evening, the last flight due to land at Nutts Corner, Vanguard G-APEF from London, had been diverted to Aldergrove owing to the weather. On 28 October, HRH Queen Elizabeth the Queen Mother officially re-opened Aldergrove as a civil airport and inaugurated the present terminal building, which is now somewhat hidden underneath subsequent development work.

British Eagle Bristol Britannia, G-ARKA, *Good Fortune. (Stephen Finney Collection)*

British Eagle Timetable. *(Guy Warner Collection)*

LONDON—BELFAST

EG 1905	Flight Number		EG 0900
Brit.	Aircraft		Brit.
Daily exc. Sat.	Frequency		Daily exc. Sun.
F/T	Class		F/T
19.05	dep	LONDON	arr	10.15
20.20	arr	BELFAST	dep	09.00
	Operates 1 April to 31 Oct.		

Belfast Schedule for British Eagle. *(Guy Warner Collection)*

BRITISH EAGLE INTERNATIONAL AIRLINES

ADVANCE TIMETABLE SUMMER 1964

1st APRIL—31st OCTOBER

Member of the International Air Transport Association

The hitherto unchallenged monopoly of BEA on the prestigious and profitable London Heathrow route saw the introduction of competition with the advent of a service by British Eagle International Airlines on 4 November 1963, using ex-BOAC Bristol Britannia four-engine, 124-seat turboprops, the first of which was G-AOVB. Both first and tourist class seating was offered, with great emphasis being put on in-flight service, including hot meals.

In its only full year of operation, 1964, over 13,000 passengers were carried but the licence restriction to a single return service a day proved to be uneconomic for the airline, which midway through the year replaced the graceful Britannias with Viscounts. After services being suspended for most of 1965, operations ceased early in 1966.

A Derby Airways DC-3 overhead Enniskillen in 1964–1965. *(Hayden Lawford)*

British Midland Canadair Argonaut at Aldergrove. *(Stephen Finney Collection)*

British Midland DC-3, G-ANTD. *(Stephen Finney Collection)*

Before changing its name to British Midland Airways, Derby Airways flew services from Aldergrove for a few months in 1964 to three destinations: Luton, Carlisle and St Angelo, Enniskillen. In all cases DC-3s were used. The first commercial service to St Angelo was on 13 March 1964, when the DC-3, G-AOFZ, landed with a charter party of anglers from Kegworth in Leicestershire. Glasgow–Enniskillen was commenced on 2 July. The first scheduled flight from Belfast to Enniskillen was on 20 July. Belfast–Enniskillen operated on Mondays and Wednesdays, with Glasgow–Enniskillen on a Thursday. The connection to St Angelo terminated on 14 October 1964. Load factors Glasgow–Enniskillen had been rather better than on the Belfast route. Burnaston was a grass field and was totally unsuitable for modern airline operation and so on 1 April 1965, BMA transferred to the newly built East Midlands Airport at Castle Donington. The first service to Aldergrove on the opening day was with a DC-3 G-AOFZ to be followed a week later with the inaugural turboprop on the route, Herald G-ASKK. A third type followed on 16 April, the Canadair C-4 Argonaut G-ALHY, which was a 70-passenger version of the Douglas DC-4, powered by four Merlin engines.

The venerable DC-3 flew passenger services for British United from Belfast to Blackpool in the mid-1960s. *(Raymond Burrows Collection)*

BKS Ambassador, G-AMAC. *(Stephen Finney Collection)*

BKS resumed its Edinburgh service on 11 May 1964, using the Ambassador G-ALZT, then added Teeside to its range of destinations on 12 April 1965, the first flight being flown by Ambassador G-AMAC, which then continued to Dublin. This route was maintained for about 18 months.

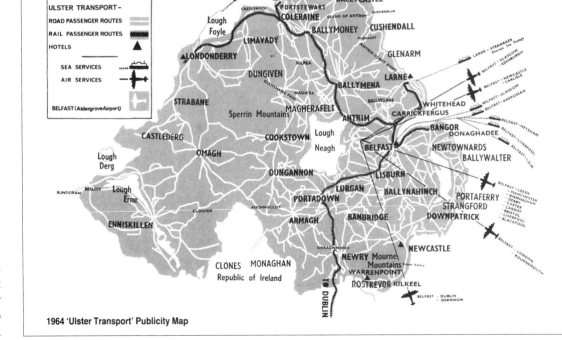

A map from the Ulster Transport Authority timetable 1964. *(via GI Millar)*

Aldergrove, as featured in the magazine *Air Pictorial* in 1966.

BOAC VC-10, G-ARVE, seen at Heathrow in 1972. *(Lars Söderström)*

Another airline flying the VC-10 from Aldergrove was British United, seen here is G-ARTA and also BEA Viscount, G-AOJF on 2 August 1969. *(John Barnett)*

On 13 August 1965 BOAC made a demonstration visit to the airport with the beautiful Vickers VC-10, G-ARVE. Its arrival was a promise of the potential of Aldergrove for services to North America. Whilst the VC-10 could indeed fly into and out of the airport, the take-off requirement with a full load of fuel and passengers did really require a longer runway to fly direct services to North America. In the meantime it was decided to provide connecting flights to the transatlantic airports at Prestwick and Shannon.

Emerald Airways DH Heron, G-ALZL, at Eglinton. *(Hugh McGrattan)*

Emerald Airways DC-3, G-AMWV, at Aldergrove. *(John Barnett)*

Emerald Airways' first service to Glasgow by DH Heron, G-ALZL. *(Hugh McGrattan)*

Emerald Airways Short Skyvan, G-ATPF. *(Stephen Finney Collection)*

25 September 1965 saw the maiden flight of Northern Ireland's first local airline, Emerald Airways, with its opening schedule flown by DH Heron, G-AOZN, from Aldergrove to Prestwick. It also used Short Skyvans and later, DC-3s. On 2 July 1966 Emerald began the first scheduled passenger service from Eglinton, the former naval air station near Londonderry, to Prestwick followed by Aldergrove –Eglinton–Glasgow–Eglinton–Aldergrove on 16 September 1966. Operations had ceased by November 1967.

British United Airways BAC 1-11, G-ASJA, at Aldergrove. *(John Barnett)*

BUA ▶
BRITISH UNITED AIRWAYS

InterJet

Now More Frequent Flights!

LONDON - BELFAST
LONDON - DUNDEE
LONDON - EDINBURGH
LONDON - GLASGOW
LONDON - GLENROTHES

Valid 1st April 1970 — 31st October 1970
Subject to alteration without notice

Timetable for British United Airways.
(Guy Warner Collection)

BEA DH Comet, G-ARGM, at Aldergrove.
(John Barnett)

1 January 1966 was the start of the first regular jet service, by British United BAC 1-11, from Aldergrove to Gatwick. As an interim measure, BEA rose to the challenge, with the introduction of the occasional DH Comet 4B to Heathrow, however, Aldergrove's runway at that time was really too short for regular use by this type.

BEA HS Trident 1c, G-ARPB, at Aldergrove. *(Stephen Finney Collection)*

HS Trident Two, G-AVFJ, at Aldergrove. *(John Barnett)*

On 16 January 1967 the 100-seat HS Trident 1c, G-ARPC, of BEA started services from Aldergrove to Heathrow. This was a two-class service with eight first class seats. The Trident had three Rolls Royce Spey jet engines and could cruise at 600 mph. Though a solid, well-built machine, the Trident's design was too closely tailored to BEA's requirements, which limited its sales appeal. It also gained the nickname of 'The Gripper' – particularly on a wet runway, it was said to take-off only due to the curvature of the earth. One record created by the Trident has, however, lasted for many years and may never be beaten, the fastest chock-to-chock time between London and Belfast of only 41 minutes.

British Midland Viscount, G-BMAT, at Aldergrove.
(M Steenson)

Also shown at Aldergrove is British Midland
Viscount, G-ASED. (Stephen Finney Collection)

British Midland Airways enhanced the service on the East Midlands route on 21 February 1967 with the introduction of the Vickers Viscount, the first schedule being flown by G-ASED, so starting an association of airline, route and aircraft type that was to last some 20 years. The first effect was to allow the frequency and capacity of the Belfast flights to be doubled.

Far left: Looking down on the check in area at Aldergrove in the 1960s. *(Belfast International Airport)*

Left: The view from visual control room, air traffic control, Aldergrove in 1963. *(Raymond Burrows Collection)*

Aldergrove from the air in the 1960s. *(Guy Warner Collection)*

Since the very first week of operation there had been complaints that the facilities provided at Aldergrove were not big enough. A works programme, costing £400,000, was started in 1966 with the result that by October of the following year, two extra bays had been added to the terminal building, doubling the departure lounge and baggage areas, increasing the size of the restaurant, providing eight more check-in desks and extra office accommodation, with the added bonus of a much improved spectators walkway. The flow of movement through the building was also improved by segregating incoming from departing passengers. To this was added an extension to the BEA cargo terminal, which doubled the space available. As well as experiencing a growth in passengers, the airport had also become quite an attraction for the casual visitor, an outing to the airport being a weekend treat for many an Ulster family of the time. The Lough Neagh restaurant provided a silver service meal and a fine view of the ramp and runway. Staff at that time have distinctive memories of their own canteen, situated at the start of what is today the international pier – famed for its soda and sausage baps as well as being the nerve centre for news and gossip.

BEA Armstrong Whitworth Argosy, G-ASXM, being loaded at Aldergrove on 23 December 1969. *(John Barnett)*

BEA Argosy, G-ASXO. *(Stephen Finney Collection)*

Caledonian Bristol Britannia, G-ASTF. *(Stephen Finney Collection)*

Transatlantic 'affiliated charter' traffic was operated by several airlines, including the Bristol Britannias of Caledonian Airways, Transglobe Canadair CL-44s and Saturn Airways Douglas DC-7Cs. The affiliated charter scheme was a means whereby a sporting or social club or society could travel at a group discount rate. It was very popular, though perhaps not all the club members were as active as they could have been – tales of 'motorcycling grannies' belonging to TT clubs are doubtless exaggerated. Another new type of aircraft made its debut on 1 April 1968, the Armstrong Whitworth Argosy freighter for an all-cargo BEA service between Belfast and London. The Trident did not have the enormous underfloor capacity of the versatile Vanguard and the Argosy had to make up the difference. It was a very distinctive aircraft with twin tail booms, a bulbous opening nose and clam shell doors to the rear.

Pictured at Dublin, the Aer Lingus Boeing 707 EI-AMW, *St Laurence O'Toole*. (Aer Lingus)

BOAC Vickers VC-10, G-ASGK, receiving the attentions of the ground servicing staff at Aldergrove on 18 July 1969. (John Barnett)

Air Ulster DC-3, G-AGJV, at Aldergrove on 7 July 1969. (John Barnett)

Though the runway was not long enough to allow for direct non-stop transatlantic services, both BOAC and Aer Lingus were able to begin scheduled operations to New York via Prestwick and Shannon respectively. Aer Lingus upstaged BOAC by four days, when its Boeing 707, EI-AMW, departed on 23 May 1968 with a passenger list including the Lord Mayor of Belfast, William Geddis, followed on 27 May by the first VC-10. Not to be outdone and to highlight the prestige aspect, on board the first VC-10, G-ARVG, was the Prime Minister, Terence O'Neill. To begin with the routeing was London–Belfast–Prestwick–New York twice weekly. Later, Belfast became the terminal point, the aircraft turned round there and did not operate through London. At the same time a feeder flight to Prestwick was maintained by the DC-3s, G-AMJU *Derry Maid* and G-AMWV *Ulster Maid* of Air Ulster, which had arisen from the ashes of Emerald Airways.

Air Ulster Vickers Viscount, EI-APD.
(Stephen Finney Collection)

Air Ulster DC-3, G-AMWV, and British United BAC 1-11, G-ASJC, taken at Aldergrove on 6 August 1968. *(John Barnett)*

The inaugural Air Ulster schedule had been flown by G-AMWV on 8 April 1968 to Glasgow. A service was also offered on the route Londonderry (RAF Ballykelly rather than Eglinton)–Glasgow–Edinburgh. During 1968, the airline also operated on behalf of British United on many Isle of Man and Blackpool flights. Later, Air Ulster leased the Viscount, EI-APD, from Aer Lingus between July and November 1969. Sadly the company could not compete on an economic basis and in 1970 met the same fate as Emerald Airways.

Autair Handley Page Herald, G-APWB.
(*Stephen Finney Collection*)

British United Island Airways Handley Page Herald,
G-APWH, at Aldergrove on 11 July 1969. (*John Barnett*)

Cambrian Viscount, G-AMOJ, at Aldergrove on 18 April 1968. (*John Barnett*)

BUA Herald, G-APWF, at Aldergrove on 17 September 1968, note
the spectators on the viewing gallery. (*John Barnett*)

Another small airline, Autair, began operating for a time to Teeside (with its terminal designed by Aldergrove's architect, WH McAlister) and on to Hull (Brough), using Heralds. This aircraft type was also flown by British United Island Airways (BUIA) to Exeter, Southampton and Blackpool – which was the new name for British United (CI) and British United (Manx). In the autumn, BKS and Cambrian swopped two routes, with BKS henceforth serving Liverpool and Cambrian flying to Edinburgh. Before that, BKS had introduced the Bristol Britannia on to the Newcastle service, with the first flight being flown by G-APLL on 3 April 1968.

World Airways Boeing 707 at Aldergrove in 1970. *(John Barnett)*

A Worldways Canada Boeing 707 awaits the arrival of the passenger steps at Belfast International. *(Tony Moore)*

A British Midland Airways Boeing 707 at Aldergrove in 1982. *(via Norman Lindsay)*

On 22 June 1968, a Boeing 707 N375WA of World Airways made the first transatlantic jet flight under the banner of the Ulster Maple Leaf Club. This remarkable travel organisation, which introduced the concept of air travel to many Ulster people, had its origins in the Belfast Tradesmen's Social Club, founded in 1955 by James Murphy. Its first flight to New York had been in 1958 from Nutts Corner, 'hopping' across the Atlantic in an Argonaut in 23 ½ hours.

Later destinations made available from Aldergrove included, not only Toronto and New York but also Los Angeles, Seattle, Orlando, Montreal and Vancouver. Aircraft used ranged from 707s and DC-8s to widebody DC-10s, Tristars and 747s. Perhaps the greatest benefit of Ulster Maple Leaf Club was the opportunity it gave to re-unite families and to allow far-flung relatives to meet for the first time.

Woodgate Britten-Norman Trislander at Belfast International Airport in 1995. *(Guy Warner)*

Early Woodgate aircraft, a Piper Aztec and two Piper Cherokees at Aldergrove. *(Guy Warner Collection)*

An early advert for Woodgate. *(Belfast International Airport)*

Later Woodgate brochure. *(Guy Warner Collection)*

Woodgate Aviation in the early days, note the Piper Cherokee. *(Stephen Finney Collection)*

Woodgate Aviation was created by the former Emerald Airways pilot, Mike Woodgate, as Ulster's first air taxi company in April 1969, at Aldergrove. He began from a base at Stand 9 on the end of the pier, with two light aircraft, a twin-engine Piper Aztec, G-ASFG, and a single-engine Piper Cherokee, G-ATWO. His brief was simple, he would fly anything, anywhere – provided it would fit into his aircraft and was within their radius of operation.

He also offered more specialised flying training than could be provided by local flying clubs. Following Mike Woodgate's retirement, Woodgate Air Charter has continued to fly from Belfast International Airport in the hands of Allan and then Johnny Keen carrying out air ambulance transfers, ad hoc charter work, aerial photography, pleasure flying, aircraft maintenance and flying training.

A composite image of BEA Vanguard, G-APEA, at Aldergrove. *(Tony Moore)*

JD Melrose. *(Belfast International Airport)*

BEA Viscount, G-AOHT, at Aldergrove. *(John Barnett)*

A newly formed company, Northern Ireland Airports Ltd, took over operation of Aldergrove on 1 June 1971 from the UK Department of Trade and Industry. The shareholders were the Treasury and the NI Department of the Environment. The financial terms negotiated were very favourable, as the runways, buildings and services were transferred to the Holding Company free of charge. This allowed the airport to function free of any burden of initial debt. The first Airport Director was already in post having succeeded Airport Superintendent John Selway earlier that year. Destined to hold that post for the next 12 years, his name was JD 'Dougie' Melrose. Formerly a WW2 Lancaster pilot, he had been awarded the DFC and had subsequently been the director of Luton Airport. A man of strong opinions, who was not afraid to express them, his influence over the next decade in Aldergrove's history was to be immense.

FOUL-WEATHER FRIENDS

BEA delighted with first diversion to Shorts' airfield

BAD visibility and a low cloud base at Aldergrove on the morning of August 23 resulted in the first BEA diversions to Shorts' airfield. Captain F Hughes flying G-AVFG, a Trident 2 with 80 passengers on board, made the inaugural landing when he touched down at 1039 hrs. He was closely followed by a second Trident and a Vanguard before visibility improved sufficiently at Aldergrove to allow normal operations to be resumed there. A Trident with a full complement of passengers left Shorts' airfield for London within the hour.

These were the first civil airliners on scheduled service to use the company's airfield for 25 years, recalled BEA Northern Ireland Manager John Swann. 'The last scheduled flight – a Dakota, I believe – left here on November 30, 1946'. He was delighted with the smoothness of the operation, the details of which had already been worked out with chief test pilot and airfield administrator Don Wright last May. He was also impressed with the quality of Shorts' technical services, marshalling and refuelling, airfield security and the high degree of co-operation with BEA ground staff.

Said Captain Hughes, 'There were no problems. Ulster radar gave us all the help we needed, then the local flight control people took over'. Mr G Plank, BEA's station superintendent, said, 'It took only 20 minutes from touchdown for the passengers to reach the city centre'.

Fog at Aldergrove caused a second diversion on September 9 when five aircraft operated by Caledonian/BUA, Northeast, Scottish BEA and BEA London were accommodated.

Shorts' house journal recorded the events of 23 August in some detail. *(Short Story, Bombardier Belfast)*

BEA Vanguard and a pair of Tridents diverted to Belfast Harbour Airport on 23 August 1971. *(Bombardier Belfast)*

Trident G-AVFJ lands at Sydenham on 10 February 1970. *(Bombardier Belfast)*

On 10 February 1970 a BEA Trident 2, G-AVFJ, landed briefly at Sydenham to assess the runway's suitability as a possible interim alternative to Aldergrove. Then on 23 August 1971 another Trident 2, G-AVFG, with 80 passengers on board, landed there. It was closely followed by another Trident and a Vanguard, the aircraft having been diverted due to bad visibility and a low cloud base at Aldergrove. Shorts carried out the marshalling and refuelling, impressing the BEA Northern Ireland Manager, John Swann, with their efficiency. Ulsterbus provided a shuttle to the city centre. Further passengers were ferried down from Aldergrove for the departure within the hour of one of the Tridents, fully loaded, to London. A fortnight later, similar problems resulted in a repeat of the process, this time involving five aircraft from Caledonian/BUA, Northeast Airlines (BKS renamed), as well as BEA again. After a gap of some 25 years, scheduled flights had once again landed at Belfast Harbour Airport.

BEA Scottish Airways Viscount at Aldergrove on 1 August 1971. *(Raymond Burrows)*

A Sterling Caravelle at Aldergrove in 1971, with a VC-10 close behind. *(Stephen Finney Collection)*

However all this lay in the future, work on the runway extension at Aldergrove was well in hand and events on the airfield over the year continued to develop promisingly. Nowhere looked brighter than the charter side, with the now usual big jet operations across the Atlantic and European services with Air Spain Britannias, Caledonian/BUA 1-11s and Dan-Air DH Comet 4s. The most intriguing route was that flown by Sterling Airways, using twin-engine Sud Aviation Caravelles to fly to Toronto and New York. Sterling's 99-seat Super 12F models flew the Atlantic from Belfast via Keflavik in Iceland, where the passengers enjoyed a five-course meal during the stopover. The elegant Caravelle was to be a familiar sight in Ulster skies in the livery of more than one charter airline for more than a decade – the most prominent of which was to appear soon, the Spanish company Aviaco.

The Short Skyvan G-AZRY which brought the Secretary of State to Aldergrove. *(Bombardier Belfast)*

Dan-Air DH Comet 4, G-APDJ, at Aldergrove on 1 August 1971, note the Army Air Corps Scout in the background. *(Raymond Burrows)*

BOAC Boeing 707 taking off from Aldergrove. *(Stephen Finney Collection)*

Following the introduction of direct rule, the first Secretary of State for Northern Ireland, William Whitelaw, was appointed in March 1972. One of the happier duties he had to perform in the midst of a turbulent year was in October, when he arrived at Aldergrove in the Short Skyvan, G-AZRY, for the official opening of the extended and widened runway. The opportunity had also been taken to install new airfield ground and approach lighting.

The occasion was graced by two Boeing 707s, G-APFJ of BOAC and G-AXRS of the recently renamed British Caledonian. Sadly there were no direct scheduled transatlantic flights to set the seal on the day, as both BOAC and Aer Lingus had stopped their big jet operation over the winter period. BOAC would not resume but Aer Lingus continued scheduled services to New York and Boston via Shannon until 1974.

Belfast Airport security. *(Victor Patterson)*

The security situation worsened and in the spring of 1973, the Provisional IRA declared Aldergrove to be a 'legitimate target'. Car bombs and rocket attacks followed, fortunately without loss of life. The aim of the terrorists was to destroy the airport, in this they did not succeed but massive disruption was caused. In order to ensure the security of staff and passengers as far as humanly possible, the terminal was closed to all except those working there, travelling or members of the security forces. Relatives and friends could come no further than the car park. An exhaustive manual search was made of all passengers and their luggage before they could enter the terminal. Check-in two hours in advance of departure became the accepted practice. Wooden and canvas structures were hastily erected to provide some rudimentary shelter from the Northern Ireland summer (normally wet). During this very difficult and frightening period no praise can be too high for the staff and indeed for the majority of customers, who coped stoically and with generally good humour. Christmas and Easter were particularly fraught, with the careful and time-consuming examination of many articles, including well-wrapped packets of soda bread being 'smuggled' back to the Mainland.

An area the public does not see, the baggage sorting and distribution basement. *(Tony Moore)*

Left and above: Check-in at Aldergrove in the 1970s. *(Belfast International Airport)*

The upper level passenger concourse at Aldergrove in the 1970s. *(Belfast International Airport)*

The famous names of BEA and BOAC were replaced on 1 September 1973 by British Airways (BA), which pre-dated the formal final cessation of these two corporations on 31 March 1974. The effect on Aldergrove's new BA route structure was dramatic, with no less than 12 destinations now being served – Heathrow, Manchester, Birmingham, Newcastle, Liverpool, Leeds/Bradford, Isle of Man, Glasgow, Prestwick, Edinburgh, Bristol and Cardiff – with Viscounts, 1-11s and Tridents. The Prestwick service was operated between 1972 and 1976 by the chartered Cambrian Airways Viscount 700 series, G-AMOG and G-AMON, fitted out in spacious fashion with only 54 seats and painted in the stylish BOAC livery until the merger. Sadly, the British Caledonian operation to Gatwick ceased, as the company was faced with a need to re-structure and cut costs, the last flight being flown by the BAC 1-11, G-AWWZ, on 31 October 1974. The next day the service was resumed by British Midland, using the faithful Viscount, G-AZLT. This was BMA's third route to add to East Midlands and the Jersey summer schedule which had commenced on 19 May 1973 with another Viscount, G-BAPG.

A British Airways Tristar taxies at Belfast International. *(via Norman Lindsay)*

An Aviaco DC-9-32 at Aldergrove in July 1982. *(via Norman Lindsay)*

There were several highlights in 1975. On 1 January, the first widebody scheduled service by BA from Aldergrove to London Heathrow was operated by Lockheed Tristar G-BBAG (which brought 230 passengers and returned with 291. Hand baggage was put into plastic bags at Heathrow to be given back to the passengers on arrival in Belfast. When faced with some 300 items encased in bin liners, quite a scrum evolved, eventually leaving the staff amidst a sea of black plastic. The system worked a little better with the introduction of see-through wrapping). This was followed by the arrival of the first Russian jetliner to make a noisy entrance (and even louder take-off), a TU-134A, YU-AJA, of the Yugoslav airline Aviogenex, bringing a football team on 14 April. A more embarrassing landing was made by an Aviaco DC-9, EC-CGQ, on 25 May, due to the Captain mistaking the old wartime airfield of Langford Lodge, just a few miles closer to the Lough, for Aldergrove.

Tridents at Aldergrove operating the British Airways Shuttle in the 1970s. *(Belfast International Airport)*

Two British Airways Tridents on the apron at Aldergrove in the late 1970s. *(Belfast International Airport)*

An Aer Lingus Boeing 747 takes off from Aldergrove in June 1981. *(via Norman Lindsay)*

British Airways' great innovation of the 1970s was the Shuttle – this provided a guaranteed seat without prior reservation to any full fare passenger who reported by a stated time – with a readiness to operate a back-up aircraft to carry those full fare passengers, however few, who could not be accommodated on the first aircraft. The service was on a definitely no-frills basis with minimal cabin service. The Belfast-Heathrow launch was on 1 April 1977, with a Trident 3B, G-AWZG. The Shuttle was a success, notching its first million passengers in the space of two years. Aer Lingus notched up a first on 3 July, with the Boeing 747, EI-ASI, *St Colmcille* beginning a short series of Maple Leaf charters to Toronto via Shannon, this being the first time a 'Jumbo Jet' had operated from Aldergrove. British Midland introduced a jet to the Gatwick route on 12 September, the leased DC-9, OH-LYB, *Darley Dale*. The flight time was thus reduced from 1 ½ hours to 55 minutes.

When Dana won the Eurovision Song Contest in 1970, she was brought home by this Aer Lingus 737, which landed at RAF Ballykelly, note the Shackleton in the background.
(City of Derry Airport)

A Loganair Timetable cover.
(Guy Warner Collection)

TIMETABLE
1st April 1979 – 27th October 1979

A Loganair publicity leaflet of 1979 featured these images of its aircraft.
(Guy Warner Collection)

Shorts SD3-30

Trislander

Twin Otter

Islander

Londonderry City Council took over responsibility for running the airfield at Eglinton following the demise of Emerald Airways in 1967. For the next dozen years there was little activity apart from some General Aviation movements and the operations of Eglinton Flying Club. April 1979 saw the commencement of a Loganair service linking Eglinton to Glasgow. Then in 1979 a summer-only weekend service connecting Glasgow with Enniskillen was inaugurated by the same company. This operated for three years, using Britten-Norman Trislanders. The first flight, however, was made by the Twin Otter G-BBLA.

A night view of the apron at Belfast International Airport in the early 1980s. *(Belfast International Airport)*

Loganair advert. *(Guy Warner Collection)*

NLM Fokker F.28 with a British Midland DC-9 in the background. *(M Steenson)*

An Aer Lingus BAC 1-11 at Belfast International in the early 1980s. *(via Norman Lindsay)*

By 1980, the Viscount fleet operated by British Airways was in need of replacement. A decision was taken by the airline that instead of making the huge capital investment to re-equip the fleet, unprofitable routes would be dropped. Several of these directly concerned Aldergrove. The Liverpool and Isle of Man services had already been passed to British Midland in October 1978, while the small Scottish airline, Loganair, had commenced on the Prestwick route and some Edinburgh services in July 1979. Now British Island Airways was to take over Leeds/Bradford (this airline was soon to be amalgamated with Air Wales and Air Anglia to form Air UK), whilst Newcastle, Bristol and Cardiff would be served by Dan-Air.

Another major development was the first scheduled connection to a European city, which was started by NLM Cityhopper, a subsidiary of the Dutch national airline, KLM (this lasted until October 1999, with the last service being flown by KLMuk). April 1980 witnessed several firsts: the initial Air UK schedule to Leeds/Bradford on the 1 April, flown by the Fokker F.27 Friendship, G-BDVT, followed the next day by the Dan-Air HS 748, G-BEBA, to Newcastle, Bristol and Cardiff, then on 8 April the NLM Fokker F.28 Fellowship, PH-CHD, to Amsterdam. The year also witnessed the ending of the Aer Lingus Shannon feeder, which had been maintained with BAC 1-11s.

British Airways introduced the 195-seat Boeing 757 on the Heathrow Shuttle service in February 1983. *(M Steenson)*

BA Concorde at the International Pier.
(Tony Moore)

2 February 1983 saw the first use of the Boeing 757 by BA, G-BIKB *Windsor Castle*, on the 8.30 am Aldergrove to Heathrow Shuttle. This was the first flight, carrying fare paying passengers, made by a type entirely new to British Airways, the 195-seat Boeing, which was powered by twin Rolls Royce RB.211 turbofans. It was also one of the first commercial jets to feature a 'glass cockpit', where the traditional rows of analogue instruments were replaced by a few electronic, high-definition colour display screens. Two of the passengers arriving in Belfast that morning were the Chairman and the Chief Executive of BA, Sir John King and Colin Marshall. Aldergrove itself was rebranded as Belfast International Airport. On 28 May, Concorde arrived in Belfast for the first time in the form of G-BOAE of BA.

A Loganair Shorts SD3-30 lands as the Spacegrand Twin Otter taxies out at Belfast Harbour Airport on the opening day in February 1983. *(Belfast Telegraph)*

One of the aircraft flown by Avair on the service to Dublin was this Shorts SD3-30, EI-BNM. *(Malcolm Nason)*

A typical scene at Belfast Harbour Airport in the mid-1980s. *(Guy Warner Collection)*

The smaller airlines and aircraft plying short distance routes did not fit in with the international image and this lack of harmony was exploited by Shorts with the re-opening of the Harbour Airport to regular scheduled passenger operations on 7 February 1983, with flights by the Spacegrand DHC-6 Twin Otter, G-BGMD, to the Isle of Man and the Loganair Short 3-30, G-BGNA, to Glasgow. So, the inaugural flights of 1938 were, by fortunate coincidence, repeated some 45 years later. The airport would offer lower aircraft landing fees, encourage the smaller airline and provide an alternative to the traveller, thus increasing competition and lowering fares. Another enterprise which benefited was Shorts itself, which was able to sell its SD3-30 and SD3-60 (later known as the Short 330 and Short 360) mini-airliners to the new and growing airlines which used its facilities at Sydenham, including Jersey European, Loganair, Manx and Avair.

A British Airways 1-11 and a British Midland DC-9 at Belfast Harbour Airport on 17 April 1984. *(Belfast Telegraph)*

Inside the rudimentary terminal at Belfast Harbour Airport in 1983. *(Bombardier Belfast)*

The entrance to the security check at Belfast Harbour Airport, shown here on 22 June 1983. *(GBBCA)*

In April 1984 Belfast International was closed for three days due to a strike and services were diverted to Belfast Harbour, which did the fledgling business no harm at all. The staff had to cope with an influx of British Midland DC-9s and Viscounts, British Airways Tridents and Dan-Air BAC 1-11s, as well as the assortment of aircraft that flew Aldergrove's nightly freight and newspaper runs.

Piper PA-31 Navajo Chieftain, G-JAJK, of Woodgate Air Charter. *(Guy Warner)*

This United African Airlines Bristol Britannia flew from Aldergrove in June 1980 with a consignment of meat destined for Libya. *(via Norman Lindsay)*

This AW Argosy, G-APRN, of Air Bridge Carriers suffered a mishap at Aldergrove in April 1982. *(via Norman Lindsay)*

Loading an Air Bridge AW Argosy at Belfast International in the mid 1980s. *(Belfast International Airport)*

In contrast to these high profile activities, the unspectacular but very useful nightly cargo work from Belfast International went on to the tune of more than 20,000 tonnes a year. It was divided into three main types, general freight which was handled for many years by the Vickers Merchantmen of ABC Carriers, newspapers flown by ABC Argosys, Air UK Heralds and F27s, British Air Ferries Viscounts and Air Atlantique DC-3s, and Royal Mail services using Air Ecosse Embraer Bandeirantes, Jersey European Twin Otters, Woodgate Pipers and Air UK Heralds. Scheduled passenger flights could also, of course, carry hold cargo.

British Midland DC-9-32, G-BMAM, at Belfast International in April 1984. *(via Norman Lindsay)*

Dan-Air BAC 1-11, G-ATPL, at Belfast International in 1989. *(Guy Warner)*

British Midland DC-9-15, G-BMAA, at Belfast International in the mid-1980s. *(via Norman Lindsay)*

British Midland was given a licence to operate on the lucrative Heathrow route from 26 March 1984, thus providing a challenge to the monopoly enjoyed by BA/BEA for nearly 20 years, since the demise of British Eagle. The high standard of cabin service offered by BMA using the smooth and comfortable DC-9 jets was a major threat to BA's dominance. The inaugural flight was made by the DC-9 G-BMAI. BA's response was the 'Super Shuttle' which included the provision of a cooked breakfast on morning flights, a free bar and complimentary newspapers. The Gatwick route vacated by BMA was taken over by Dan-Air with BAC 1-11s in February.

Official programme for the Air Fair Spectacular 1984. A major article in this publication on the history of Aldergrove was written by Ernie Cromie. *(Guy Warner Collection)*

The Air Fair Spectacular included the Red Arrows in its list of attractions. *(Belfast International Airport)*

On 17 August 1984 the airport hosted the first flying display to be held at Aldergrove for 21 years, the 'Air Fair Spectacular', which included the Red Arrows, the RAF Falcons parachute team, an Avro Vulcan and Concorde in an impressive show. The event was planned as a family day out for all, with any profits being donated to organisations benefiting the blind and was the brainchild of the airport's Chief Executive Gerry Willis. Over the years, very successful civil airshows have also been held at Newtownards, City of Derry Airport, Portrush and Newcastle, as well as fly-ins organised by the Ulster Flying Club at Ards and the Ulster Aviation Society at Langford Lodge and Maze/Long Kesh.

The view from apron control. *(Belfast International Airport)*

The new apron control tower under construction at Belfast International in the mid-1980s. *(Belfast International Airport)*

A British Airways BAC 1-11 on stand at Belfast International in 1988. *(Belfast International Airport)*

The completion of the final part of Belfast International's 10-year plan in 1986 saw the international pier improved and a much needed extension to the cargo ramp. But the most dramatic change was to the main building with the demolition of the original finger pier, which had simply become too small to handle the increase in passenger numbers and aircraft size. BA and BM (no longer BMA, having dropped the Airways in 1985) were placed at each extremity of the terminal with nose-loading 'airbridges' so that passengers would no longer have to venture outdoors to progress from lounge to aircraft. In between and forward of the check-in hall, an eight-sided glass fronted structure provided more holding lounges and viewing gallery for spectators, friends and relatives. This marked the final rehabilitation of the visitor to the airport who had been re-admitted on a limited basis since 1978. Atop the new edifice was an apron control room, giving airside operations an excellent vantage point.

Piper Chieftain G-OLLY of Robertson's Foods at Belfast International in the mid-1980s. *(via Norman Lindsay)*

A Cessna 500 Citation parked in front of the Executive Jet Centre. *(Belfast International Airport)*

In 1987 the Executive Aviation Terminal opened with Belfast International being marketed to the operators of business jets as the most westerly airport in the UK with full Category III landing capability, which allowed precision instrument approach and landing to suitably equipped aircraft. In the same year passenger figures at Belfast International exceeded 2,000,000 for the first time. Over at Belfast Harbour, the passenger figures climbed through the 200,000 mark to 279,000 by the end of 1987. In a very competitive market, the concept was surviving and developing its customer base.

A TU-134A of the Yugoslav airline, Aviogenex, arrives at Aldergrove in 1982. *(via Norman Lindsay)*

An IL-18V of the Romanian airline, Tarom at Belfast International in the 1980s. *(via Norman Lindsay)*

Balkan Bulgarian Airlines IL-18D at Belfast International in 1984. *(via Norman Lindsay)*

Aviogenix Boeing 727-200 YU-AKM at Belfast International in July 1985. *(via Norman Lindsay)*

A Tarom TU-154 at Aldergrove in July 1982. *(via Norman Lindsay)*

Over the years, aircraft enthusiasts have always welcomed visits to Northern Ireland by Eastern European airlines, which tended to operate rarely seen Russian types. Here is a selection of these, with one 'Joker'.

The Loganair BAe 146, G-OLCA, at Belfast Harbour Airport. (*Raymond Burrows*)

Manx Airlines Short 360, G-SALU, at Belfast Harbour Airport. (*Ernie Cromie*)

Easter 1989, the Stranmillis College badminton team departs for Paris in a Fokker F.28 of TAT. (*Guy Warner*)

On 1 August 1988 the first regular jet operations from Belfast Harbour began, with the Loganair BAe 146-200 G-OLCA (though the first 146 to land was a one-off extra flight by a Manx Airlines aircraft on 30 April). Further improvements were made to the airport's infrastructure with Ulster Aviation Fuels (Air BP) and Inflight Catering Services setting up bases on site. Meanwhile at Belfast International, Air France subsidiary TAT began a scheduled service to Paris on 31 October, which lasted for a couple of years.

The old control tower at Belfast Harbour Airport. *(Belfast Telegraph)*

A Jersey European BAe 146, Manx ATP and in the background, a Loganair ATP at Belfast City. *(Guy Warner Collection)*

The entrance to Belfast City Airport. *(Bombardier Belfast)*

In 1989 Belfast Harbour Airport was renamed Belfast City Airport. A major new programme of capital investment in equipment and facilities was initiated, prompted by the continuing rise in passenger numbers. The schemes set in motion in this year included the provision of new instrument landing systems, surveillance radar equipment, a new aircraft parking apron, a greatly enhanced terminal building, a fleet of fire rescue vehicles and a state of the art Air Traffic Control tower, which was designed to incorporate the

Fire Station. Some unwelcome attention came later that year with a terrorist bomb attack causing damage to the control tower. A single fast-moving brick ripped through all the communications lines except the link to Aldergrove's tower. The staff worked a minor miracle in clearing up the mess, as did British Telecom in repairing the lines and also the Air Traffic personnel at Belfast International, who guided aircraft towards the City Airport. Within a very few hours the City's tower was functioning fully again.

Shown here on the runway at Belfast International is the British Midland Boeing 737-400, G-OBMF, which is a sister-ship of the aircraft which crashed at Kegworth. *(Raymond Burrows)*

On 8 January 1989, the British Midland Boeing 737-400, G-OBME, en-route from London to Belfast on the evening BD92 service, developed engine problems which resulted in an attempted emergency landing at East Midlands Airport. Tragically, the aircraft just failed to reach the runway and instead impacted on an embankment at the verge of the M1 Motorway at Kegworth. 47 people were killed and 78 injured. This accident had a deep impact on the staff at Aldergrove, as many of the victims were well known as frequent flyers.

Dan-Air HS 748, G-BFLL, at Langford Lodge on 3 March 1989. *(Pacemaker Press)*

Shown here at its correct location, Belfast International Airport, is the Dan-Air 748, G-BFLL. *(Raymond Burrows)*

On 2 March 1989, a Dan-Air HS 748, G-BFLL, on the DA141 service from Newcastle with 29 passengers on board landed at Langford Lodge by mistake. This was before the establishment of the museum by the Ulster Aviation Society there, which was perhaps fortunate for the airline, as some of the enthusiastic members might have wished to add the 748 to the Society's aircraft collection. As it was, the passengers proceeded to Aldergrove by bus, while the aircraft flew out empty.

Britannia 737-200,
G-AXNB, at Belfast
International Airport.
(M Steenson)

Air UK Fokker F.27 at Belfast International. *(Tony Moore)*

Dan-Air BAe 146-100, G-BKMN, at Belfast International in the 1980s.
(via Norman Lindsay)

On 8 December 1989 Britannia Airways, which was much better known for holiday charter flights, began a scheduled service to Luton from Belfast International using Boeing 737s, with a very attractive fare of £29 single. This was well ahead of its time and can be regarded as the first 'low-cost' operation to Belfast. It lasted for five years.

This Beechcraft King Air, EI-BFT, was flown by Avair. *(Malcolm Nason)*

Aer Arann operated this Piper PA31, G-WSSC. *(Malcolm Nason)*

Eglinton timetable from the early 1990s. *(Guy Warner Collection)*

Shannon Executive operated this Swearingen Metroliner, EI-BRI. *(Malcolm Nason)*

Iona Embraer Bandeirante, EI-BVX. *(via Paul Duffy)*

Meanwhile throughout the decade, Eglinton had been making progress with a route to Dublin being operated in turn by Avair, Aer Arann, Shannon Executive, Iona and Aer Lingus Commuter. In addition, Loganair had continued to serve Glasgow from 1979 and had also operated to Blackpool and the Isle of Man for a few years, while commencing a service to Manchester in 1989.

The Iona timetable for 1988 shows an ambitious Irish route structure. *(via Michael Traynor)*

A busy cargo ramp at Belfast International.
(Guy Warner)

The new cargo centre at Belfast International in the early-1990s. (Belfast International Airport)

Further construction at Belfast International was begun in 1990 with the start of work on a new cargo centre, while the East Terminal Extension gave upgraded and improved passenger facilities. Both BA and BM were provided with new, enlarged departure lounges, BM also gaining a new check-in. A more modern and spacious baggage reclaim area was added and the departures concourse was extended, as was the viewing gallery. The project lasted some 16 months and was divided into 14 separate phases to ensure that the disruption to airport operations was kept to the minimum. The new cargo centre at Belfast International was officially opened on 17 July 1991. It was designed to offer the user a fully integrated range of freight handling services with an extensive, dedicated aircraft apron, adjacent terminal, freight yard, handling agents, customs brokers, forwarding agents and express transport operators all co-located on the same site. Its worth was to be seen early in the following year, with the formation of the Post Office Skynet next-day mail distribution system, which re-organised the existing postal network and saw Belfast connected nightly with Liverpool, East Midlands, Stansted, Bristol and Edinburgh.

The new hotel at Belfast International Airport in the early-1990s. It has undergone several changes of ownership and name over the last 20 years and is now the Maldron Hotel. *(Belfast International Airport)*

Cessna 550 Citation II, G-JFRS, at the Executive Jet Centre. *(Raymond Burrows)*

In June 1993, the 108-bedroom Novotel Belfast International Hotel was opened to the public. It also provided a restaurant and bar, a conference and banqueting suite and a fitness room and sauna. Being situated some 60 metres from the main terminal entrance, it could hardly have been more convenient. To complement this construction, the exit and entrance hall was much improved and a canopy was provided over the set down and pick-up areas, considerably improving the overall first impression on arriving at the airport. Inside the terminal, the catering and retail outlets were overhauled, as was the check-in hall. No doubt these improved facilities also impressed travellers using the Executive Jet Centre.

A Jersey European BAe146 prepares for take off at Belfast City Airport. *(Guy Warner Collection)*

Three Jersey European BAe 146s at Belfast City Airport. *(Guy Warner Collection)*

Important developments at Belfast City included in April 1993 the start of Jersey European's BAe 146 service to London Gatwick and early in 1994, the opening of the very smart new combined Air Traffic Control and Fire Station. That year passenger figures exceeded 1,000,000 per year for the first time.

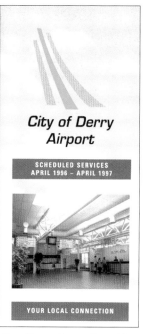

City of Derry Airport timetable from the mid-1990s. *(Guy Warner Collection)*

Aerial view of City Of Derry Airport. *(City of Derry Airport)*

The first arrival at the new City of Derry terminal in 1994 was a Loganair Short 360. *(City of Derry Airport)*

29 January 1994 saw the opening of a new terminal at Eglinton, the first arrival with passengers using the new facilities was the Loganair ATP, G-LOGG. In the same year the airport was renamed City of Derry. Jersey European operated a route to Dublin for a few months in 1995.

Passengers disembark from British Airways (Maersk) BAC 1-11 at Belfast International Airport in the mid-1990s. *(Guy Warner)*

Belfast International was being hurt badly by the competition from the City Airport which, however, could not take over routes which required large aircraft as its runway was not long enough nor could it provide the round-the-clock opening hours essential for freight and holiday flights. It was against this rather gloomy background that in February, Parliament passed the Airports (Northern Ireland) Order 1994, which enabled the Belfast International to be privatised by way of a trade sale. On the credit side, it was a business that could hardly fail, as an international airport is an essential part of any country's infrastructure. There had been considerable investment of government and European cash to enhance and modernise the facilities, while the long-term growth potential of commercial aviation is vast. On 20 July 1994 a management buy-out for the sum of £32.75 million resulted in the creation of Belfast International Airport Holdings Ltd.

HT&H Jet Ranger, G-CORT.
(Raymond Burrows)

Robinson R22, G-KEVN, of Helicopter Training
and Hire at Belfast International Airport.
(Guy Warner)

On the General Aviation front, Helicopter Training and Hire (HT&H) moved to Aldergrove from its former base at Newtownards. Over the following months it was to develop considerably, with the construction of purpose built facilities to house the aircraft; providing maintenance, classroom and office accommodation. A full range of rotary-wing activity was being offered from training to commercial pilot standard, to corporate and personal business or pleasure flying, as well as aerial filming and photography. The growing fleet started with the basic, two-seat piston engine Robinson R22, to which were added the gas turbine powered Agusta Bell 206B Jet Ranger, G-CORT, and the four-seat Robinson R44. HT&H were to be joined soon by another helicopter operator, Eurojet, with another Jet Ranger, G-ISKY.

BA (Brymon) Dash-8, G-BRYS, at Enniskillen. *(Gerry Gallagher)*

BA (Brymon) Dash-8, G-BRYV, at Enniskillen in 1999. *(Gerry Gallagher)*

Crossair Saab 2000, HB-IYG, at Enniskillen in 1999. *(Gerry Gallagher)*

Crossair Saab 2000, HB-IYB, at Enniskillen. *(Gerry Gallagher)*

Starting on 24 June 1995 Brymon Airways/BA Express flew summer schedules from Enniskillen to Jersey. The Bombardier Dash 8 was the largest type at that time to operate a regular passenger service from the airport. The inaugural trip was flown by G-BRYH. This was followed on 21 June 1997 by Crossair which began a summer charter series from Enniskillen to Zurich with the Saab 2000, HB-IZM. The passengers were given a VIP reception, as this was the airport's first direct link with Europe.

Some of the aircraft which brought President Bill Clinton and his entourage to Belfast International Airport. Clockwise from top left they are VC-25A 28000, a C-137, a C-5 and a VH-60. President Clinton has, of course, been followed on visits to Northern Ireland by George W Bush and, most recently, Barack Obama. *(Raymond Burrows)*

Following the terrorist cease-fires, the US President and First Lady, Bill and Hilary Clinton arrived in Northern Ireland on 30 November 1995 to add their weight to the peace process. Not only Air Force One VC-25A 29000 (an executive conversion of the Boeing 747) arrived at Aldergrove, it was accompanied by a considerable collection of other first-time visitors to the Province, bearing security staff, limousines, helicopters, the Presidential entourage and a large media contingent. These included the back-up VC-25A, two C-137s (military 707s), three massive C-5 Galaxy transporters, the press corps 747 of Tower Air and four helicopters – two VH-60 Seahawks, one MH-53 Sea Dragon and a CH-53 Super Stallion. The sight and thunderous sound of the helicopter formations crossing Belfast Lough and passing along the Glengormley Gap was a particular memory of an important few days.

An aerial view of Belfast International Airport in the mid-1990s. *(Belfast International Airport)*

Lockheed Tristars of Air Transat flew transatlantic services from Belfast International in the 1990s. *(Paul Harvey)*

TBI became the new owners of Belfast International Airport on 13 August 1996. The Editor of the *Ulster Airmail* greeted the announcement with cautious optimism, "The news that Belfast International Airport has been bought in a £107m deal by the property and leisure group TBI, owners of Cardiff Airport, has generated much comment on the government's £33m valuation two years ago and envy of the good fortune/foresight of those able to take part in the management buy-out who now see their investment being returned more than a hundred fold." The long transition from being what was effectively a public utility to becoming a wholly business oriented enterprise was nearly at hand.

Hunting Cargo Airlines Vickers Merchantman, G-APEP, at Belfast International Airport in 1996. *(Guy Warner)*

Parcel Force Vickers Viscount, G-OPFI, at Belfast International Airport. *(Guy Warner)*

30 November 1996 saw a very sad farewell, the final departure by the last surviving Vickers Merchantman, G-APEP, *Superb*, which in its earlier guise as a BEA Vanguard had been flying into Belfast since 1963 – a remarkable career. 8 January 1998 brought the final departures from Belfast International of the British World Vickers Viscounts G-AOHM and G-OPFI, resplendent in their red Parcel Force livery. Another link with the first day of operations in 1963 was gone. Now only the cargo-carrying Fokker F.27 and the occasional ad-hoc DC-3 survived as types that had visited the terminal on day one, 35 years before.

easyJet Boeing 737, G-EZJB, lands at Belfast International Airport. *(Paul Harvey)*

Passengers disembark from easyJet 737-300, G-EZYF, at Belfast International Airport. *(Guy Warner)*

18 September 1998 saw the first of the new breed of 'low-cost' operators beginning operations at Belfast International, the easyJet service to London Luton, with Boeing 737-300 G-EZYG.

An unusually sedate shot of Ryanair CEO, Michael O'Leary at City of Derry Airport on 4 May 1999. *(Photocall Ireland)*

Ryanair Boeing 737 EI-CKQ.
(Michael Kelly)

1 July 1999 brought the first Ryanair service from City of Derry to Stansted by Boeing 737-200, EI-CKQ. An proving flight by EI-COB had brought Ryanair's ebullient CEO, Michael O'Leary to the airport a couple of months earlier. The next few years would bring significant growth with services to Liverpool, Prestwick and East Midlands being inaugurated by Ryanair, as well as connections to Manchester and Birmingham with Aer Arann and also a programme of holiday charter flights to a variety of European destinations.

Dash-8, G-JEDY, of British European at Belfast City. *(Paul Harvey)*

Go 737-300, G-IGOA, departs Belfast International Airport. *(Paul Harvey)*

The year 2000 brought four significant developments. In May, Jersey European announced that it was changing its name to British European and in June came the first use by BA of the latest and smallest member of the Airbus family A319, G-EUPJ, on Belfast International to Heathrow. On 1 November, another 'low-cost' airline, Go, began a three times daily service on the Belfast International–London Stansted route with the arrival of the Boeing 737-300, G-IGOR. In December, an Irish Public Service Obligation (PSO) contract for Dublin to City of Derry was awarded to Loganair, which inaugurated the service on 18 January 2001 with Short 360, G-BPFN.

The airside exterior of the new terminal at Belfast City Airport. *(GBBCA)*

MyTravel flew charter services from Belfast International with A320s. *(Paul Harvey)*

Gill Airways brochure from 2001. *(Guy Warner Collection)*

2001 began promisingly with the establishment of a new international route in January by easyJet from Belfast International –Amsterdam, beginning with a single daily rotation and inaugurated by the 737-300, G-EZYL, and then the opening of the smart new terminal at Belfast City in May by First Minister David Trimble. This was to change dramatically later in the year after the dreadful events of 9/11 in New York. Gill Airways, which had been operating at the City Airport for a dozen years, ceased operations, Aer Lingus (which had been operating transatlantic services via Shannon since 1995), BA, British Midland, Sabena (which had been operating a service to Brussels since 1998) and British Regional Airlines withdrew all services from Belfast International. BRAL and BM (apart from its Heathrow schedule which operated from both airports until withdrawing finally from Belfast International in March 2003) moved flights to the City Airport. The last service by the national flag carrier from Northern Ireland was on 27 October 2001 from Belfast International to Heathrow by the A319, G-EUOF.

The control tower and terminal at Enniskillen. *(via Noel Baskin)*

Compare the size of this Ryanair Boeing 737-800, EI-DCX, with the passenger terminal at City of Derry Airport. *(Guy Warner)*

An aerial view of Enniskillen, St Angelo, taken in 2009. *(Guy Warner)*

An unusual view of a Loganair Saab 340, taken from a Royal Navy Lynx at City of Derry Airport. *(Guy Warner)*

In 2002 St Angelo, Enniskillen closed, to reopen again for General Aviation in 2004. Also in 2002 Go was bought by easyJet. There was good news for City of Derry, where both Ryanair and Loganair announced increased schedules and new destinations.

Belfast International 17 February 2007, bmibaby 737, G-TOYD. *(Guy Warner)*

On the ramp at Belfast International, a Boeing 737-700 of easyJet receives the attention of the ground staff. *(Guy Warner)*

Jet2 Station Manager, Debbie Abbott, with Boeing 737, G-CELY, at Belfast International. *(Guy Warner)*

Over the next few years a pattern began to emerge with the 'low-cost' model beginning to dominate the scene with easyJet, bmibaby (from October 2002) Jet2 (from November 2003) at Belfast International, Flybe (the new name adopted by British European in 2002) at Belfast City and Ryanair at City of Derry, to a wide range of destinations with more European cities being served than ever before. Times were tough and if a new route did not prove to be economically viable, it did not last long, so the pattern became one of swift change. Small, start-up carriers found it very difficult to gain a toe-hold in the market or even to survive. In May 2003 the Spanish company Ferrovial bought Belfast City from Bombardier for £35m.

The daily scene on the cargo ramp at Belfast International in 2012. *(Norman Lindsay)*

A hare crosses the taxiway at Belfast International Airport in 2012. *(Norman Lindsay)*

Continental Airlines Boeing 757, N57111, departs Belfast International Airport – note the large winglets. *(Raymond Burrows)*

In December 2004, Belfast International was sold by TBI to ACDL/ Abertis of Barcelona in a £551.3m overall deal for Belfast, Luton, Cardiff, Stockholm Skavsta and Orlando Sanford. There were some major developments at Belfast International in 2005. On 27 May, Continental Airlines began a service to Newark, New Jersey with the Boeing 757-200, N19117. This was the first non-stop scheduled service from Northern Ireland to the USA and it carried 85,000 passengers in the first year of operation. (Continental merged with United Airlines in 2010, with rebranding of all aircraft in the United livery in 2012). On 22 June, Zoom started flying to Halifax and Toronto, the first service being flown by the Boeing 767-300, C-GZNA. It went out of business in 2008. Flyglobespan flew to Florida and Canada from 2006–2007, until it too collapsed in 2009.

The late Dickie Best with Brian Ambrose at the official naming ceremony on 22 May 2006. *(GBBCA)*

A busy ramp scene at George Best Belfast City Airport. *(Guy Warner)*

George Best Belfast City Airport. *(GBBCA)*

On 22 May 2006, Belfast City was renamed George Best Belfast City Airport (GBBCA). Then, in September 2008, GBBCA was sold by Ferrovial to ABN AMRO Global Infrastructure Fund for £132.5m, while in October Loganair terminated its City of Derry to Glasgow service after 29 years.

A panoramic view of Belfast International Airport in 2012. *(Norman Lindsay)*

An overview of the new entrance at Belfast International, which was opened in December 2009. *(Belfast International Airport)*

Above right: A United Airways Boeing 757 taxies past at Belfast International Airport. *(Norman Lindsay)*

Right: Airbus A320, G-DHRG of Thomas Cook, which is a major charter operator at Belfast International. *(Guy Warner)*

In 2007, Aer Lingus established a base at Belfast International (including a schedule to London Heathrow from January 2008) and Ryanair began operations from Belfast City, which only lasted until 2010, the airline declaring this was due to its frustration over delay to the runway extension plans.

The ill-fated Manx2 Fairchild SA-227BC Metro III, EC-ITP, at GBBCA on 9 January 2011. *(Dave Henderson)*

A Manx2 LET-410 on the ramp at Belfast International. *(Guy Warner)*

Citywing at GBBCA.
(Paul Harvey)

On 10 February 2011 the Manx2 NM7100 service from GBBCA to Cork was flown by the Fairchild Metroliner, EC-ITP, which crashed at Cork in fog making a third attempt to land. Two crew and four passengers were killed, six passengers were injured. The service terminated in mid-March. Manx2 had begun operations from both Belfast International and GBBCA in 2006. In January 2013, following a management buy-out, the company was renamed Citywing and currently operates schedules to the Isle of Man, Blackpool and Gloucester.

King Airs from Cobham Aviation Services visit all UK airports regularly to calibrate the radar and landing systems, G-FPLE is seen here at GBBCA in 2011. *(Guy Warner)*

An unusual visitor to GBBCA in 2011, MBB Bo.105, EI-BLD, of Irish Helicopters, which was checking power transmission cables in the area. *(Guy Warner)*

bmibaby 737-300, G-TOYJ, arrives at GBBCA. *(Paul Harvey)*

31 October 2011 saw bmibaby inaugurate the first direct European scheduled service from GBBCA to Amsterdam, following its move from Belfast International.

Airbus A319, G-EUPC, of British Airways arrives with the Olympic flame at GBBCA on 2 June 2012. *(GBBCA)*

A traditional salute for British Airways A319, G-DBCH, as it arrives at GBBCA for the official launch party on 2 July 2012. *(GBBCA)*

Aer Lingus A319, EI-EPR, lands at GBBCA. *(GBBCA)*

A good variety of tail fin markings may be seen at GBBCA. *(GBBCA)*

In the spring of 2012, bmi (British Midland) was sold to the International Airlines Group (British Airways and the Spanish flag carrier, Iberia). It was announced that the bmi GBBCA to London Heathrow route would be maintained but with aircraft flying in BA livery as the year progressed. In May it was announced that bmibaby would cease operating from GBBCA in June 2012. Not long afterwards it was learned that Aer Lingus would move its entire operation from Belfast International to GBBCA at the end of October. A boost to the Northern Ireland civil aviation scene was given in November 2012 when it was announced that Air Passenger Duty (APD) on long-haul flights from Belfast would not be levied from January 2013 onwards.

The Squirrel, G-SWEP, which crashed in the Mournes. *(Guy Warner)*

EC-135, G-PSNI, at Aldergrove. *(Guy Warner)*

The original RUC Islander G-BSWR *(PSNI)*

Three PSNI helicopters, EC-145, G-PSNO, BK-11? G-DCPA and EC-135, G-PSNI *(PSNI)*

The original Police Air Support Unit (ASU) was formed in 1993 as part of the Royal Ulster Constabulary (RUC). It was equipped with a single Britten Norman BN-2T Islander, G-BSWR. It was found that air support was most often needed by Traffic Branch, the Drug Squad, CID, the Photographic Unit and for public order duties (for example, parades). Valuable assistance was also given to a number of other agencies, including the Coastguard, HM Customs and Excise and the DoE. Over the years since the formation of the ASU, awareness of the capabilities of the aircraft and the practical benefits that air support brings has risen steadily. Accordingly, the requests for aviation assistance have steadily grown and the hours on task have increased proportionately from 300 in the first year to several times that amount today. In 2001 the RUC GC was renamed the Police Service of Northern Ireland (PSNI). Further aircraft were added to its strength, Eurocopter EC-135T2, G-PSNI, in 2005, Eurocopter AS355 Twin Squirrel, G-SWEP, in 2009, Eurocopter EC-145, G-PSNO, in April 2010 and to replace G-SWEP, which crashed in the Mourne Mountains in October 2010, Eurocopter BK-117, G-DCPA. Taskings have increased year-on-year by a steady 10%, with some 3600 in 2011–2012. The Unit consists of a Detective Inspector, four Detective Sergeants, 18 Detective Constables (organised in three sections) and a dozen pilots. It is based in a purpose-built complex at Aldergrove.

George Wynne-Eaton, Resident Instructor of the Ulster Flying Club in the 1950s. *(Guy Warner Collection)*

The Ulster Flying Club's three Tiger Moths at the start of a day's flying in 1954. *(Guy Warner Collection)*

Sir Douglas Bader opening the new UFC clubhouse at Ards in 1975. *(Tommy Maddock)*

Aircoupe G-AROO was used by the Ulster Flying Club as a trainer in the 1960s. *(Tommy Maddock)*

Ulster Flying Club Cessna 172S Skyhawk, G-UFCE, at Ards in 2012. *(Guy Warner)*

Owner-pilot, James McMeekan and G-AROO at Ards in 2012. *(Guy Warner)*

In 1951, Shorts took over the airfield at Ards and sponsored the Flying Club which resumed flying operations in 1953, with DH Tiger Moths. A few years later McCandless Aviation set up engineering works in the hangars and took over running the Flying Club from Shorts. The Ulster Flying Club was re-formed in 1961 and since that time has had responsibility for the airfield, training thousands of students to fly, organising Air Rallies and promoting Air Shows. A new clubhouse was opened by Group Captain Sir Douglas Bader in 1975. Following its destruction by fire in 2004, a fine replacement was completed and opened by HRH the Duke of York in 2005. It is now one of the largest flying organisations in Ireland, providing a wide range of aviation services and training.

Aero-Heli Robinson R.22, G-BOCN, at Ards in 2012. *(Guy Warner)*

Aero-Heli Robinson R.44, G-OORM, at Ards in 2012. *(Guy Warner)*

Rotary-wing flying training has been conducted at Newtownards and Aldergrove. The first company to offer this was Helicopter Training and Hire in the 1990s with Robinson R.22Bs. Aero-Heli, which is based at Ards, offers flying training, pleasure flying, sightseeing, corporate travel, aerial filming, wedding transport and private hire. Currently helicopter operations are also provided by Cutting Edge at City of Derry and Sloane at Enniskillen. Other companies which operated helicopters in Northern Ireland included Eurojet Aviation at Aldergrove with a Bell 206 JetRanger III and Heli-Trans at Belfast City with an Aerospatiale AS350 Squirrel, G-BMAV. There are also of course a number of privately owned helicopters, several of which have taken part in Ulster Aviation Society Fly-ins at Maze/Long Kesh.

1931/32 – the UGC's first primary glider. A single-seat trainer that was catapulted down a slope, not usually gaining much altitude. The instructor shouted commands by megaphone. Here seen at the Holestone flying ground near Templepatrick. *(Carl Alexander Beck via Tom Snoddy)*

The UGC's airfield at Bellarena, Co Londonderry. *(via Tom Snoddy)*

This Schleicher ASK-21 glider, G-CKOT, is currently in service with the club, seen here soaring over Binevenagh mountain about two miles from the airfield. *(via Tom Snoddy)*

Billy Reed at Gallion. *(Ulster Hang Gliding and Paragliding Club)*

Ian Cross at Magilligan. *(Dave Tweedie)*

The Ulster Gliding Club was founded in August 1930. Early activities took place at Comber, Ballymiscaw, Doagh, Tyrella, Templepatrick, Knockagh and Magilligan. After the end of the Second World War, gliding recommenced at Magilligan, Limavady, Maghaberry and Long Kesh. Launches were made by the reverse-auto-tow or pulley method. This employed an old Bedford barrage balloon truck as anchor point for the pulley around which piano wire was pulled by a powerful car. Initially the car was a straight-eight Buick followed by a variety of ex-MOD war surplus staff cars, some of which were still painted in their desert colours. The main tow-car from 1965 up to the time the club was obliged to vacate Long Kesh was a 1954 Cadillac Fleetwood. This 5.25 litre V8 monster, weighing in at about 2.5 tons, was capable of 0 to 60 in 10 seconds which was very fast in those days. A privately owned Auster Terrier aircraft was made available for occasional aero-tows. In 1970 the club vacated

Long Kesh at the urgent request of the Ministry of Defence and moved to Ards for seven years and then to Bellarena in 1978, finally moving 1000 yards to the north in 1993, where it has remained to this day, with all single and two-seat glider launches aero-towed by Robin DR300 or Piper Super Cub.

The Ulster Hang Gliding and Paragliding Club was formed in 1990 when it incorporated foot launched paragliding, having been the Ulster Hang Gliding Club since 1975. It comprises some 68 pilots who fly from a mixture of inland and coastal sites throughout the Province, from a suitable hill facing the prevailing wind on the day, arrangements having been made with a number of landowners scattered throughout the country who kindly gave, and continue to give, permission for flying from their land. Of course in order to protect everyone's interests, third party insurance cover for all members and the landowners is in place.

Joanne Snoddon prepares for a flight. *(Gerry Snoddon)*

A Quik 912S at Ards. *(Ernie Cromie Collection)*

Thruster T600N, G-CGFZ, prepares for take-off from the grass at Ards. *(Ernie Cromie Collection)*

Gerry Snoddon, a CAA Instructor Examiner and an IAA Instructor Examiner, one of the most experienced microlight pilots in Ireland, writes, "In the early 1980s several local pilots bought and tried to fly microlights. Most of the aircraft were beefed up hangliders with all sort of different power plants, ranging from cement mixers to snowmobiles. This carefree experience brought a very poor reputation of accidents. This in itself brought about the British Microlight Aircraft Association that started to govern the sport for the CAA. The BMAA then formed a council which in turn trained the most experienced pilots to become Flying Instructors. This made a big difference to the accident rate and overall safety. At present microlight pilots in the Irish Republic are trying to get themselves organised and several of the local instructors at Newtownards from Northern Ireland Microlights are giving them a hand, using the experience that they have gained from the CAA and from instructing from Ards for the last 25 years or so. There are about 50 microlights now based at Ards and almost double that scattered around the Province. Some of the trips that have been made from Northern Ireland have been down to central France for the Blois microlight gathering and local pilots from Ards have even flown the Dambuster route down to the Ruhr valley. The aircraft today are much more capable than those flown by the microlighters at Ards when they first took up the sport. The Irish Aviation Authority has licensed Ards as one of only four licensed microlight training schools in Ireland and the only one north of the border."

Parachutists board the Cessna 208 Caravan 1, G-ETHY, at Movenis. *(via Trevor Taylor)*

Ulster Aviation Society member, Trevor Taylor, with his instructor, Alan Davies, receives his certificate after completing a tandem parachute jump for charity. *(via Trevor Taylor)*

Two miles outside Garvagh in Co Londonderry, is the airfield of Movenis. It is the home of the Wild Geese Parachute Centre and was opened in 1983 by Dave and Maggie Penney. The main purpose of the airfield is acting as the main base for sports parachuting in Northern Ireland, which attracts some 3000 jumpers annually, some of whom make 200–300 descents a year. Training is conducted by British Parachute Association registered instructors in a 13,000 square feet hangar, which was constructed in 1990 and has all the necessary aids – including two mock-up fuselages and six fan trainers (this involves jumping off a platform to simulate a landing). In the early days, jumping was undertaken from Cessna 182s but as the centre has gained in popularity, so more capable aircraft have been employed, such as the Cessna Caravan. Ulster Aviation Society member, Trevor Taylor, made his first jump at the age of 76 in October 2012, raising more than £2000 for the Friends of the Cancer Centre in the City Hospital, Belfast.

INDEX